—16—
PILLS

16 Pills

Carley Moore

TINDERBOX EDITIONS

Tinderbox Editions
Molly Sutton Kiefer, Publisher and Editor
Red Wing, Minnesota
tinderboxeditions@gmail.com
www.tinderboxeditions.org

Cover design by Nikkita Cohoon
Cover photograph by Jackie Dives
Interior design by Nikkita Cohoon
Author photo by Amy Touchette

For Malka, my fellow dreamer

CONTENTS

16 Pills

THE SICK BOOK

Hospital Time

I was nine and away from home for the first time. There was a schedule, a plan, but I wasn't in on it. I started to understand the weird rhythm of doctors—the way they're never around when you need them or always with another patient or worst of all, in surgery. I went to appointments I didn't know had been scheduled and always without my parents, who were two hours away at their jobs. I began to cultivate irrational fears: *the orderly will lose me and I'll never see my parents again, the nurse will forget to tell my parents I'm having a brain scan and they'll leave without seeing me,* or *somehow my roommate and I will become separated and I'll have to sleep alone.*

For Example

Like the time I couldn't get my underwear on. Like the time I wore a body stocking and got painted in plaster. Like the time I was carried home from the zoo. Like the time everyone was way too nice to me at the birthday party. Like the time I fell off the bleachers. Like the time I ate gravel. Like the time I stepped on a bottle cap and someone's older brother carried me home bleeding. Like the time I couldn't walk across the lawn. Like the time when I got extra Valentines from a classmate for being "special."

Pediatrics

My room had still aquarium-like lights and nurses who came in every hour. My sheet felt thin against the hot, dry air. I read my first mystery about a smart boy who wrestled with a falcon and a weathervane on the roof of a church. When I was allowed, I walked to the gift shop and fingered the stuffed animals. Later, during visiting hours, I dropped hints to my parents. "That little penguin is really cute," and "Did you see that sad elephant?" I skidded around the floor in my standard-issue hospital socks. I was more mobile than most kids, at least in the morning.

My Roommate

Like Jane Eyre, I had a beautiful roommate who was dying slowly. She had a pixie haircut and an attentive and ever-present mother who arranged framed family photographs on the radiator. At night she whispered in her sleep. Nothing I could ever make out. Was it wrong to see her as already dead? Like all good idol-friends, she was blonde, bony, and chic even in her gray-green hospital gown.

Braces

The orthopedist worked out of the hospital basement. My parents came for the fitting. I could feel the doctor eyeing me when I put on a body stocking. I was mortified by its transparency, the way it clung to my stomach and thighs. He told my father to get a shotgun, to keep the boys away. "She's that kind of pretty," he said. I wasn't buying it. I'd met dirty old men before, knew their tricks. But we needed him, so we sat there grim as the concrete wall. The braces were molded out of plastic, made hard in a kiln, and shaped to fit the bottom of my foot, my heel, and the back of my calf. The strap was a thick strip of industrial-grade Velcro that made my leg red and sweaty. There was no quiet way of taking them off. I hated them instantly and I knew they wouldn't work.

Judy Blume

Deenie was my favorite book. The heroine, a girl with scoliosis, must learn to accept her brace. But she was so obviously a caterpillar-to-butterfly kind of girl. It was unclear what I was becoming.

Transference

My neurologist was glamorous. She wore high heels with her white lab coat. I could hear her walk down the hall towards my room, calling out to her favorite nurses by name. She carried a flashlight pen and tested my reflexes by running the sharp tip of her house key along the sole of my foot. I hated her for that instant of pain but immediately forgave her. She would cure me — I could tell. "Kiddo," she said, day after day, "could you walk down the hall for me?"

Spinal Tap

I wanted my mother with me, but she wasn't allowed in the room. Instead I got the usual efficiently sweet nurse, who I knew was just doing her job. *You can't possibly love me*, I thought as she rubbed my forehead with her soft thumb. She asked me to count to ten. When I got to seven, she gently took off my underwear. I thought, *I shouldn't be awake for that*, and then suddenly I wasn't.

Optometry

The orderly wheeled me into the waiting room of another weird basement outpost and receded back into the elevator with a nod. I admired the height of his afro, but I didn't say anything. I didn't know if we were supposed to talk. I got out of my wheelchair to look around. The waiting room was empty, and there was no receptionist. My fear of being alone slowly transformed into boredom. I stood on the chairs and spun the eye-malady pamphlet rack around until it nearly toppled. I ripped two pages of lion pictures out of a magazine and stuck them in my robe pocket. I called down the hall twice, a faint, "Hello?" I pressed the elevator button, watched the elevator door open and close revealing no one and nothing. Finally, a doctor appeared, nose to clipboard, mumbling, "Yes, yes, you must be next."

Video Tape

I was a puzzle. I walked down hospital hallways while visiting doctors leaned against the wall to watch. Sometimes they exchanged information about me. *You say she's worse at the end of the day?* Or asked a question. *Why does the left side drag more than the right?* But they never spoke to me. I started to hate hallways—the slippery waxed floors, the sheer length of them, and the way they shaped my sense of myself as spectacle. Some days I walked better than others. Some days, especially late in the day, I couldn't walk. On those days, one of the doctors gave me his arm for support. I focused on his watch or the tuft of wrist hair poking out from beneath his shirtsleeve, anything to not look at his face. Near the end of my stay, someone—a resident—videotaped me. I never understood what that tape was for—a record of embarrassment, a way into an unknown archive, a testament of sorts?

More Gift Shop

I liked the stationery sets and postcards, which suggested that hospital time was really just a vacation. I wanted the mug with a rainbow on one side and a plump heart on the other. The silver "Get Well Soon!" balloons seemed to float on the air of their own certainty. I even liked the red t-shirts with the hospital's logo on them. The powdery old ladies who volunteered in the gift shop sold individual postage stamps and monitored the helium machine. They favored hot pink lipstick that clung to their front teeth and wore blue striped smocks over their loose polyester blouses. One even let me work the tiny register while she went outside for her afternoon cigarette.

The Boy

His room was at the end of the hall, farthest from the nurses' station. He had cancer or a bad heart, something that might kill him. We played crazy eights in the afternoon, always in his room. He couldn't get up; he was attached to machines. I noticed his skinny ankles, his feet bare and chapped. I imagined us on the outside—riding skateboards and getting matching haircuts.

Field Trip

Right before Christmas, the nurses arranged for a small group of us to leave the hospital and see *A Christmas Carol*. We left in a black van with a broken heater, packed in with extra regulation blue hospital blankets. There was snow on the stage and a flying bed! Afterwards, lying in the hospital bed staring up at the fluorescent light, I wondered how I'd been chosen for the trip. *Did my parents sign me up? Did they fill out a permission slip?* Maybe I wasn't as sick as I thought.

Discharge

I didn't say good-bye to my roommate or the boy. They were both at appointments, and I didn't ask to wait. My father carried my light blue suitcase with the snap latches to the long-term parking lot while my mother talked about my brother who was at home building me a fort. It didn't occur to me to ask questions. Nobody ever knew anything anyway. I was leaving. That was enough.

Reward

After I got out, my parents gave me a plaid diary with a tiny matching plaid pen. I wrote my first entry about my stay in the hospital. I stuck to the facts (room decor, nurses' names, and length of stay) and shared it at the dinner table while my brother ran a Matchbox car back and forth across the length of his placemat. I didn't think then that a diary should be a record of feeling, so I didn't write about the night the nurse came in to check on me because I was crying. I thought I was asleep. I thought I was only dreaming of crying.

After

I extracted promises at awkward moments. When my mother was drying my hair, I shouted over the roar of the hairdryer, "I don't have to go back, right?" She smiled weakly and started to use the brush to straighten my bangs. I slammed the door of my father's car and said into the January air, "I'm done with hospitals." My father looked across the hood of our blue, rusting Volvo and nodded. One January afternoon, when my brother threatened to break the leg of my favorite Barbie, I said to him cool as a spy, "No matter where I go, you can never have my room."

ON UNHAPPINESS

I started reading Jennifer Senior's *All Joy and No Fun* on the eve of my daughter's sixth birthday party. I'd been eyeing the book in the bookstore for a couple of months and my boyfriend sent me her Ted talk when the book first launched. From the Ted talk and the landscape of my own parenting—I'm a separated, co-parenting mom, a writer and an academic, who tends to struggle between two internal voices—I was pretty sure the book would speak to me. I worry, overbook, and fret about how M. is fairing in relation to her peers, as a child of divorce, as an only child, as a child without much of? financial safety net, and then when I exhaust myself doing that, I chill out and opt out of a lot.

M's birthday is in July, which meant we'd already cycled through a full year of birthday party celebrations with her classmates. I understood, early on, that these parties were part of what I jokingly started referring to with M's dad as "the birthday industrial complex." They are serious business. One family rented the Intrepid. Another treated all of the girls in the class to pedicures, manicures, and up-dos with a *Frozen* karaoke backdrop. There were tea parties in fancy restaurants, dance lessons, gymnastic parties, I could go on.

And we go to public school. Granted, it's in the West Village of New York City where, according to New York City census data, the median income in this neighborhood was $112,689. I make about two thirds of that, and the reason I live in this neighborhood is I've taken a position in my university that allows me to live an apartment in a residence hall. It's a temporary position (lasting anywhere from three to nine years depending on my performance), and though I have long-term teaching contracts separate from my position in the dorm, I do not have tenure and I am not eligible for long-term faculty housing. I know I am lucky to have my position, but I live paycheck to paycheck with no savings and no plan for future housing.

I looked into it and most of these parties cost between $800 to

$1000. M's dad and I don't have that. We were already tapped out from paying for summer camp. I also wanted desperately to model a different kind of birthday party for my child and for other parents. We'd have it in the playground of Washington Square Park, there would be pizza and a homemade cake, and the kids would run around. I sent out the evite. *No biggie. I got this.*

My first sign that the party might suck was that almost all her classmates were out of town. *So sorry, we're in Italy for the summer. Wish M. a happy birthday! We'd love to come but during the summer we spend our weekends in Montauk.* Several parents never responded to the evite at all. M's friends from outside of school were also away. Her de-facto godmother, a party staple and one of our closest friends, was caring for her wife's sick father. As the weekend for the party approached, we had only five guests. The forecast said rain. I prepared M. for the possibility that the party would be very small. M. said she didn't care, but as she ticked off the list of her friends at school, and I said, "No, she's away. No, he can't come. No, she's away too," I saw her face fall and set in that determined, heart-breaking, soon-to-be-six-year-old-way.

I was also, I knew, repeating old patterns with my ex, ways of behaving that had doomed our marriage and I sometimes still clung to. I felt he was not doing much for this party so I doubled my efforts. I ordered a gross of *Frozen* party supplies from Amazon. I baked the best cake I could manage—it took four hours and another adult to help me decorate it, but I was determined! I was clearly trying to prove something to myself, to my kid, to these parents I was secretly envious of and also mad at for setting the bar so high, and for making birthdays into a contest I could never, ever win. I knew something had come unhinged, when I cried (not my daughter, but me a 42-year-old woman) in front of *Party City*. Our Elsa balloon bumped up against the jagged corner of an overhang and popped. I special ordered it from Amazon, and *Party City* almost wouldn't fill it with helium because they hadn't sold it to me. I begged and the stone-faced teenager behind the counter relented with a long-winded hate sigh. She was right. I hated me, too.

I remembered reading the chapter called "Marriage" in *All Joy and No Fun* the night before. Even though we were separated, I was often looking to do some kind of a post-mortem on the corpse of my marriage. Would this text give me more data or insight into understanding how we went wrong? Much of it resonated—how a small child destabilizes a marriage, the different ways in which fathers and mothers care for young children, and the mother who does way, way, way too much. I saw myself, in my birthday party mania, in one of the mothers Senior writes about, Angie, who constantly wonders if she's doing enough and doing it right. Senior admits:

> But perhaps one of the hardest and most elusive quantity for a time-use survey to measure is the physic energy that mothers pour into parenting—the internal soundtrack of anxieties that hums in their heads all day long, whether they're with their children or not (59).

I knew that soundtrack. I was listening to it every minute lately. On repeat.

As for my own marriage, as sure as I was that we'd done the right thing for both ourselves and for M., much of what Senior noticed and researched about couples struck me. I knew, especially in the last two hard years of our marriage, that my ex and I really didn't even believe in marriage anymore. We saw ourselves as shift workers more than partners, we traded off our kid, had alternating teaching schedules and very little money for child care, and so we passed each other in the night and day. Senior warns that this arrangement is a "formula for exhaustion, and it creates a scarcity economy on days off, pitting spouses against each other over who gets the easier assignments on the to-do list and who gets the spare hour for a bike ride or nap" (51).

My ex, it turned out, helped with the party quite a lot. He came over early and decorated the apartment. He bought the pizza and went with me to Party City to buy favors and decorations. He hugged me in front of *Party City* when I lost it over the balloon, and I could see in his eyes that he hoped I would get a grip.

I sort of did. The party, it turned out, did suck. We managed about eight kids—four friends from school, and an assortment of old friends from Brooklyn, and a random kid I basically pulled off the street. The kids trashed my apartment and M's toys. She got stressed trying to navigate the weird social dynamics of having old and new friends together. When everyone was gone and I was down on all fours pulling bits of cake out of the rug with my hands, M. told me that "It was the worst birthday party ever." I felt a scrim of bloody rage fall over my eyes.

"No, it wasn't," I shot back. *I worked so hard!! It's not my fault!!* I wanted to shout.

"I didn't have fun!" she said.

"That hurts my feelings," I said and I saw that she was confused. Was this party about her or me?

I put on a *Tinkerbelle* movie and took some deep breaths in the other room. I texted my boyfriend who was kind and helpful and reminded me that it was okay if the party was a bust. I remembered Elsa's anthem in *Frozen*, "Let it Go," and I realized it was finally time to do just that.

After M. watched *Tinkerbelle*, I asked her if there was anything fun that happened at the party and she admitted that she loved making the cake with me and when I told everyone that she was the baker. She also loved the hour we managed in the playground before coming to my apartment for pizza and cake. I asked what she didn't like and what wasn't fun? She said, "The fighting, everyone was fighting and the boys broke things." I remembered all of my own party anxieties growing up and that I still found parties overwhelming and weird. I said, "You know it's okay that you didn't have fun at the party. Birthdays can be hard." She nodded and started writing in her "fairy field journal."

But the party—this vexed situation—that I created, but is also at the heart of modern middle-class American parenting in particular, gets at a larger thing I've been thinking about lately as a parent, a teacher, and a person. How can we make space for sadness, for bad feelings, and for being unhappy?

In one of my favorite parenting books, *How to Talk So Kids Will Listen and Listen So Kids Will Talk* by Adele Faber and Elaine Mazlish, dealing with negative feelings is central to raising healthy kids and also to resolving family conflicts. The authors write, "Steady denial of feelings can confuse and enrage kids. Also [it] teaches them not to know what their feelings are—not to trust them" (2).

I've thought a lot about this in relation to M's dad and my separation. At first, I wanted to do anything I could to make it okay for her, to relieve my own guilt and anxiety over what we were doing to her and to her family. I wanted to fix it and make it better. Thankfully, at the moment that M's dad and I were separating, we were lucky enough to be attending a nursery school that had a strong therapeutic/emotional component. At the heart of its curriculum was a belief in play and a mandate to help children express and process their feelings in a positive way. I remember one morning when I dropped M. off, several children were crying. It was just one of those days, a "sad day," as her teacher called it. M. and I looked on as the teachers comforted the kids. The mantra at that moment was, "It's okay to be sad." The teachers offered up activities after they'd let the kids cry, but mostly they just made a comfortable space for the sadness and asked questions about what was making each child sad. They didn't try to distract them from their sadness or even minimize it. M. and I both walked away from that morning with that mantra in our heads, "It's okay to be sad." M. sometimes reminds me when she's crying and it guided me through much of those first hard months of our family's split. It was sad, and it was better if I just acknowledged M's sadness over her parents' separation rather than try to pretend otherwise.

Moments like these (the failed high-stakes birthday party, my separation and future divorce, and the "it's okay to be sad" morning at the nursery school) and books like Senior's *All Joy and No Fun* and Faber and Mazlish's *How to Talk So Kids Will Listen and Listen So Kids Will Talk* make me wonder about the complicated feelings Americans have about happiness and success. Our "Declaration of Independence" states that "life, liberty, and the pursuit of happiness" are among our rights, but do we privilege happiness at the cost of other less-tidy emotions? And what do we lose out on when we ignore sadness in ourselves or in our children?

Reading Barbara Ehrenriech's *Bright-Sided: How Positive Thinking is Undermining America* and watching *Slavoj Zizek's The Pervert's Guide to Ideology* remind me that happiness is a particularly American ideology. The success of books like Rhonda Byrne's *The Secret* and Gretchen Rubin's *The Happiness Project* indicate that like most ideologies, this one functions well within the dominant structures of late capitalism. For Byrne and Rubin, happiness and the pursuit of it, is about individual self-work and our belief in ourselves as people who can change. These writers subtly embrace the ethos of the American Dream—only hard work and your own perseverance will lead to happiness. There's no examination of how social institutions and the government can intervene on behalf of citizens to make our lives better and less anxious.

This extreme focus on the self—our own and our children's happiness—can too easily encourage us to ignore the truly difficult problems that are happening all over the world. Ehrenriech and Zizek remind us that happiness or the pursuit of it is an ideological hamster wheel. We run on it, exhaust ourselves trying to get at it, and we become blinded to so much of the mayhem around us.

It was easier for me to try to create the perfect birthday party than to process the horrors in Israel-Gaza, the growing Ebola virus in Africa, and the fact that 219 Nigerian schoolgirls were still missing.

I wanted my daughter to have a "happy birthday," because, like so many American parents, I sometimes think that my ultimate parenting goal should be to raise a "happy kid," and I struggle mightily with my own political failings—do I protest enough, have I called enough senators today—and how to teach her in ways that are age-appropriate about just a fraction of what is going on in the world.

At the heart of *All Joy and No Fun* is English psychoanalyst Adam Phillips, who writes, "Happiness is an unfair thing to ask of a child. The expectation casts children as 'anti-depressants,'" and makes parents more "dependent on their children than their children are on them" (234). I suspect, too that our American obsession with happiness makes us much less likely to engage with the political realities around us. We try to focus on ourselves, on our individual happiness because the larger social political landscape is so vexing, and distinctly unhappy. Maybe our founding fathers had it wrong. Why is the "pursuit of happiness" a right?

I started reading Gretchen Rubin's *The Happiness Project* yesterday and I finished it in twenty-four hours. There's much in it I admire and agree with—making failure fun, writing a novel, making new friends, singing with your kids, fighting fair, sleeping more, and exercising better, to name a few. I admire too, her honesty about herself, her attempt to "be Gretchen" and the idea of the book project itself. What a fascinating thing to attempt! She's a diligent researcher and she makes sticker charts for resolutions complete with gold stars. And yet, I also found the book depressing, gimmicky, and ultimately exhausting. Sentences like "I am happy—but not as happy as I should be," and "I had to create a scheme to put happiness ideas into practice in my life," reminded me of the endless striving I'd done when M. was a baby to keep up with the other married folks I knew in Brooklyn (7, 13). I don't want to work really, really hard to be happy. I don't want to apply a Martha Stewart-like laser focus to it, and it troubled me that Rubin, for all of her smart and reflective willingness to tackle this huge emotion refused to try therapy and meditation, two of the things I've found the most useful in my quest for what I can really only bring myself to call stability.

And maybe I don't even want to value happiness anymore. Maybe I'm sick of trying to achieve it, which is not to say that I'm not delighted when I feel it. I am! It's lovely! Oh, that dopamine is powerful stuff! I'd like to really laugh at least once a day and go dancing every other weekend! If I had a fairy wand that worked, I'd wish a mind-blowing, endorphin-inducing orgasm on everyone at least once a day! Of course, that is, if you want one.

One of the few good things about going through a separation is that nobody really expects you to be happy anymore, at least in the early parts of it. For someone like me who has had her fair amount of childhood trauma anyway, this has felt like a glorious reset button. *Fuck it. Let's stop pretending. Happy? Let's just get through this day without crying on a student.*

Near the very end of the documentary *The Pervert's Guide to Ideology*, Zizek reminds us that the basic lesson of psychoanalysis and cinema is that, "Our dreams stage our desires and our desires are not objective facts. We created [our dreams], we sustain them, and we are responsible for them." Because of this, he argues that "the first step to freedom is not just to change your reality to fit your dreams, it's to change the way you dream." He warns us, too, that to change the way you dream is painful; freedom hurts. I'd like to stop dreaming and scheming about happiness for myself and for my daughter. When happiness comes, I'd like to enjoy it, instead of fearing that it will never return.

ON NITPICKING AND CO-PARENTING

"Where did you get that?" I stared at my soon-to-be-ex-husband as he affixed a headlamp to his forehead and our five-year old daughter wriggled off her shirt and settled into his office chair for what had to be the millionth hour of *Angelina Ballerina*.

"Duane Reade. Jealous?"

I nodded. I was impressed. Not to be outdone, I offered, "I bought coconut oil and tea tree oil. We can melt them together and slather on after we pick. I also brought my hair dryer. I heard they can't take the heat. Oh, and new hair clips to section off the hair."

"Mama, is there candy?"

"You can eat whatever you want." The only way to get a five-year-old to sit still for an hour or two of nitpicking is to stuff them with sugar and cartoons.

M. rummaged around in the brown shopping bag of lice treatment products her dad and I had been toting back and forth between our apartments for the last week, and pulled out a bag of cherry hard candies. She scratched her shoulder and returned to the mouse dance drama that was unfolding in the English town of Chipping Cheddar.

This was our second lice battle. I'd found them crawling around on M's head before Christmas and spent a disgusting six hours shampooing and combing the still kicking lice out of her hair on a Saturday night. M's dad was out of town and after I was done, I went into my bedroom, shut the door, and cried for a quick minute. I felt exhausted and overwhelmed, like I feared being a single mom would feel in the months before my separation from M's dad. This time, the school called her dad, and he called me since it was my day. We agreed to get supplies at meet-up later to nitpick. When I arrived at her school, M. had been quarantined in the cramped nurse's office with at least twenty other kids. Instead of speaking to the school nurse, I was greeted by a lice-removal salesperson, who was charging parents $1000 to comb through a child's hair and de-louse the apartment. He thrust a flyer into my hand, and turned to one of his employees.

"She's got live lice, right?"

"Yep," the young woman didn't look up from the hair of one of M's classmates as she deftly parted it with two small sticks.

M. buried her head into my leg and cried. I wanted to cry again too, but I didn't. I'd learned that in my five years of being of mom—if you're a good parent, mostly, you don't get to cry. Or you do it later, on your own, with a glass of wine or with a friend or for a quick minute in the bedroom while the Backyardigans are dancing the two-step. There was something so galling about the cold practicality of the lice removal salesman when I was hoping for the folksy comfort of a school nurse. Do public schools even have nurses anymore?

A week later, I found out from another mom in my daughter's school that she actually paid over $1300 to have her whole family combed out and nitpicked. Neither M.'s dad or I have that kind of money lying around, and if we did, we'd probably spend it on summer camp or three year's worth of school clothes or half of a shitty used car. I get that parents need help, and that many of the parents at my daughter's public school can afford these treatments. Nitpicking and lice removal are big business, especially in cities where infestation is common and there are a lot of middle-class overworked parents. I found several articles about Orthodox Jewish women in Brooklyn who had become professional nitpickers after dealing with their kids' lice. One, according to an *A.M. New York* article from 2009, Dayla Harel, has put six of her nine kids through college by nitpicking (Naanes). Most professional nitpickers are women.

Nitpicking, I'd learned, was a very particular kind of hard, focused labor. It reminded me of the kind of feminine precision work I'd failed at growing up: needlepoint and quilting. You needed good eyes, and really good light, and you needed to care. "Don't drop the stitch," I heard my mother saying gently over the hoop of a sampler I'd botched. "You have to follow the pattern," my 4-H teacher sighed into the soft light of her Singer. I was too impatient to be much of a seamstress. I refused to use the seam ripper on mistakes, instead insisting that I had my own vision, one that included dropped and crooked stitches. The results were shoddy and embarrassing. I usually stuffed them under my bed or threw them out altogether. As an adult, when I saw a quilting show of the African-American quilters of Gees Bend, Alabama, I understood the difference between improvisation and mistake. Intention. Vision. Belief. My daughter's kindergarten teacher calls a mistake that turns into something viable, a "beautiful ooops." As a young girl, I knew only patterns and rules. I wanted to be an artist, to improvise off of a mistake, but I couldn't make the leap. Mistakes were to be ripped out. They were not a riff to extend.

I found the needle arts boring, but the stakes were low. I could walk away and zone out in front of *The Brady Bunch,* which I did. Staring at my daughter's teeming, bug-infested head for that first comb out; I knew I had no choice. I had to remove every last bug. It was tedious, precision work we were too broke to pay anyone else to do. The nits are the size of a grain of sand, and you have to look on almost every hair follicle. My daughter's hair is fine and long, and as her dad and I took to calling it under our breath, "louse brown."

Around that same time, I re-watched the seminal sci-fi movie *Alien* with a friend, and because I had lice on the brain, I could only see the alien and her sticky, vicious spawn as a kind of futuristic killer lice. When part of the crew discovers the alien eggs hatching on a windy, desolate planet, I whisper-hissed at the T.V., "Oh, God no! You have to kill them all! Get every last one!!" Ash, the crew's android, admires the "purity" of the alien, its uncanny ability to survive. Lice, too, have this purity. Lice have existed since humans have, and they'd rather die than eat anything else but us.

Much has been written about the Freudian mothering that happens on that doomed spacecraft. The ship's computer is called Mother. Ripley, the sole (female) survivor, must kill the mother computer and the potentially egg-baring (s)mothering alien to live. She risks her life a couple of times to save the ship's cat, Jones, and in doing so becomes a kind of mother herself. Ripley is a bit of nitpicker, too. She senses, before anyone else, that Ash is not to be trusted, and she hectors the rest of the crew about quarantine protocol. She's a reluctant leader, an alien nitpicker, who knows she has to kill to survive. She cries, too, in her moments of fear, but these are the frustrated tears of someone who knows that she has no other choice. Ripley understands that the future of the human race is in her hands. She embodies a feminist ethos I've come closer to realizing as a single, co-parenting mom. *Get to work! Pick those nits! And be grateful that your daughter's dad is so—well—present!*

When we battled the lice, M's dad and I been separated for a year. We've since gone through mediation and now we're divorced. We are friends, we talk or text most days, and we co-parent. M's spends half of her time with each of us. He is an excellent dad and my dear friend.

When you Google the words "nitpicking" and "women" most of what comes up is relationship advice. The top hit is from Web-MD-"Want a Happy Marriage? Don't Nitpick." As I learned the true meaning of nitpicking, I thought about the ways in which I nitpicked M's dad when we were married, especially in those last two very hard years of our marriage. I suppose we picked at each other, or I picked and he withdrew. We both felt so wronged and so misunderstood!

You're bossy. You're very detail oriented. You like to be right. You cross all of your t(s). You can't let it go. You have to have it perfect. You always get your way.

I've heard these phrases from parents, friends, and even well-meaning colleagues. I suppose my ex hurled one or two of these at me, too, and I'm sure I deserved it. They are code for nitpicking, ball-busting, acting the part of the difficult woman. The nitpicker is a good foil, a scapegoat for larger struggles around relationships both at home and in the workplace. And I admit, too, that I can be difficult and exacting. But I'm also funny and sexy and smart. I may pick nits, but I am no longer that nitpicking wife!

Maybe I never was. And hey, what about Ripley? Nitpicking keeps her alive, doesn't it? Or, maybe if she could have eased up a bit on her crewmates, she might have had more help in killing that alien.

That first year of separation was hard on us all. M. was adjusting to living in two apartments and to the loss of married parents. M's dad and I were mourning our marriage and learning how to live as single adults. But I see in our relationship, in our shared quest to rid our daughter's head of vermin and our resistance to getting fleeced out of money we don't have, some core beliefs about co-parenting that are at the heart of my favorite parenting book, *Co-Parenting 101: Helping Your Kids Thrive in Two Households after Divorce* by Deesha Philyaw and Michael D. Thomas. I was drawn to this book because of its tagline, "practical advice from a formerly married couple." *Wow,* I thought. *They're divorced and they managed to co-author a book! I'll buy that!* In their introduction, Philyaw and Thomas define successful co-parenting as "any post-divorce or post-separation parenting arrangement that (1) fosters continued, healthy relationships for children with *both* parents and (2) is founded on a genuinely cooperative relationship between the parents" (6). They urge co-parents or divorcing couples that are considering co-parenting to put the kids first and to remember, "It's not about you" (9).

And so for those two weeks, M's dad and I came together to nitpick. We had two metal combs, and though we couldn't both fit around the small circumference of our daughter's head, we kept each other company, made jokes, and divided up the sections of her head. Since then we've celebrated holidays as a family and taken trips together so that M. can still feel what it's like to have two parents together in the same room.

"I'll do the bottom if you do the top." He clicked on his headlamp. M scratched at her shoulder again until it was red.

I wish to return nitpicking to its original lice hunting origins. Nitpicking is precision work, often relegated to wives and mothers, but it needn't be so. M's dad is actually better at getting the nits off of her hair than I am. His vision is sharper and he has a firmer pinch.

Lice love our company—they've evolved to capitalize on our sociability, so if we must kill them, why go it alone? In a *Scientific American* article from biologist blogger, Emily Willingham, "Of Lice and Men: An Itchy History" I am equal parts horrified and fascinated to learn, "In two Peruvian mummies dating to about 1025 CE, for example, one specimen had 407 lice on its head, while the other had 545." My first thought is, "Oh god, there are lice still on those mummies! We're doomed!" My second thought is, "I wonder if those mummies were married?"

21 + 21 = 42

On the morning of my 42nd birthday, my then-boyfriend asked me what I was doing when I was 21, half that age. I said, "Baking quiches, dropping acid, and chasing boys." I imagined this retort as a tweet—short and direct. I'd managed to get my life at that time down to 39 characters, and it was mostly accurate.

At 21 years old, I was obsessed with Molly Katzen's Moosewood cookbook *The Enchanted Broccoli Forest*. I was going to a state school in upstate New York, not far from the home of the Moosewood restaurant in Ithaca, which had always seemed to me a cultural mecca in a vast state of industrial depression and blight. Ithaca was the home of my favorite thrift shop, Zoo Zoos, and a lot of cute hippie musicians I fantasized about fucking. The cookbook was steeped in that same sexy, vintage, hippie musician lore. I imagined myself cooking for one of those musicians. *I could be his "old lady" for a recipe or two,* I thought, trying on the 70s language I'd heard my parents joke about. Many of my activities then were overlaid with a fantasy plot line, worthy of an episode of *Laverne and Shirley* or *Three's Company.* I was rarely just doing something; I was doing that thing while imagining I was in the TV sitcom version of it. As a child, I'd made it through the chore of washing the dishes by pretending I was in a Dawn dish soap ad.

My favorite pages in *The Enchanted Broccoli Forest* offered a basic crust recipe on one page and on the facing page a list of choices for quiche fillings—cheeses, veggies, and meats (if you must). It was my favorite type of recipe, more about endless iterations and the possibility of a food than its experience of it. That year, I regularly turned out a ham and cheese quiche, brown gazpacho, and rocky oatmeal bread that my roommates and I ate with a fake enthusiasm to prove to ourselves that because we could cook we were adults.

I was also dropping a fair amount of acid. I did it as one might perform a colonic or go on a silent yoga retreat. Results varied. Once,

I watched in fascination as the words I spoke come out of my mouth as giant, puffy, rainbow cartoons. It's a clear message to me to this day: *You think words are beautiful and fun.* Another time, I hallucinated a wall catching fire while one friend squeezed syrup into another friend's mouth because she'd forgotten to take her insulin shot and was having a diabetic fit. The wall, it turned out was not on fire, and our friend did not die, but I understood that action was better than just sitting and staring. Still, often when I was tripping, I stared at myself in the mirror. I found this profoundly comforting. Aside from a bit of narcissism in this act, I was mostly desperate to see myself. Not knowing who I was, I looked for clues. Tripping made it okay for me to slow down and stare at myself in the mirror. For these rare moments, I was free of self-judgment. I liked myself when I was tripping, and I was oddly calm unlike in my non-tripping life when I was stressed about relationships, my family, school, and money.

Between cooking, classes, and dropping acid, I chased boys. I started long-term relationships from one-night stands, I followed a classmate home on the bus and played dumb when he noticed me, and I drunk-dialed a semi-famous rock star from my home town because I'd heard from a friend he was into me. I'd been shamed out of masturbating to *Mighty Mouse* when I was six and I didn't really get the hang of having orgasms again until I was 20. It was at that time that I met a graduate student who knew what a clitoris was and relieved me from the elaborate performance of faking it that I thought was my fate. With a lot of catching up to do, I experienced my desire as a time bomb—explosive, ready, and manic.

Around the time I was turning 42, Tom Junod, who himself is in his late 50s, published the now much-lampooned "In Praise of the 42-Year-Old Woman" in *Esquire.* He began in this depressing way:

> Let's face it: There used to be something tragic about even the most beautiful forty-two-year-old woman. With half her life still ahead of her, she was deemed to be at the end of something—namely, everything society valued in her, other than her success as a mother. If she remained sexual,

she was either predatory or desperate; if she remained beautiful, what gave her beauty force was the fact of its fading. And if she remained alone…well, then God help her.

According to Junod, 42 used to signal the end of sexuality for women. All we 42-year-old-women had left to do was keep on being devoted moms. If we were gross enough to try to get laid, then we were predatory or desperate, and we were still pretty, it was only in that vintage way. The rest of the piece is a catalog of which 42-year-old-celebrity women are fuckable (all!) and the great news that at least feminism has made middle-age women worthy of the male gaze. The response was swift and hilarious. My favorite came from Tracy Moore at *Jezebel* who wrote:

> Why, it used to be, a woman at the age of 42 could hardly be glanced at, much less taken to bed and ravaged shame-free in broad daylight. No longer. *Esquire* has sent word across all channels that 42-year-old women have been removed from the Do Not Bang list and are no longer off-limits to respectable men. In other news, FIRE SALE AT CHICO'S.

I remembered Junod's piece a couple of months later when I bought, Anya Ulinich's graphic novel *Lena Finkle's Magic Barrel.* I've been looking for models—female characters who aren't punished or compromised by their sexuality, who are parents with desires, and who aren't necessarily on the hunt for a husband or a great love. I've been looking for artists and writers who defy conventional plot devices and narrative structures and who aren't trying to tell us that life is anything more than a series of events, some large and some small, some painful and some joyful.

The main character, Lena, is 38-year-old mother of two teenage girls and lives in Brooklyn where she works as a freelance illustrator. At 18, she emigrated from Russia to the U.S., and much of the novel is about her grappling with that original clash of cultures (Soviet deprivation and Glasnost opening up next to American abundance and the taint of late capitalism). On the first page, we see a sleeping Lena lying in front of the "Department of State" building in St. Petersburg, Russia. She's been invited back to Russia for a book tour. Lena admits, "My sexual awakening was entirely the fault of the U.S. state department" (3). The book follows Lena as she learns how to use OkCupid, negotiates a tortured decades-long romantic connection with her first love Alik, and eventually falls in love with a totally emotionally present yet completely unattainable man she calls "the Orphan." Sex with "the Orphan" is transformative, and over black and white drawings with a watercolor-esque wash of the two characters in bed, Lena confesses, "My inhibitions and long-established boundaries fell away. I no longer had any use for my escape routes…and there I was suddenly without my exoskeleton, but totally alive" (254).

I was drawn to Lena's sloughing off of her exoskeleton, her desire to be totally alive, and Ulinich's skill at creating such a complex character. Lena—to steal from my favorite psychoanalyst D.W. Winnicott-a "good-enough mother" who is not consumed by her role as caregiver. She's an artist and a teacher who is ambivalent at times about how those two jobs intersect. She enjoys one-night-stands, awkward pity sex, draws during the day, drops off and picks up her daughters from school, meets regularly with her friends Eloise and Yvonne, visits Occupy Wall Street, and shops for school clothes. Eventually, she is nearly undone by the Orphan, but at the center of the book is the journey of becoming her own person. Not a daughter. Not a mother. Not a wife. Not even a girlfriend.

I saw some of myself in Lena, her joy at discovering sex reminded me of my early manic search for a sexual connection at 21 and then again at 42. Once I'd healed a little from my separation from my ex, I made tests for myself. I learned for the first time in my life how to go to a bar and have a drink alone. I danced with strange men and got lost in the heat of a dance floor. I cut my hair short and reveled in the freedom I felt when passing as a young man or a butch woman. I set up an OkCupid account and referred to the site with my friend Stephanie as "the man store." And I, like many newly single middle-aged women and men I've spoken to, marveled at the ease of internet dating, the way you could actually know something about a person before that first awkward meeting. It was so much different than dating in my late twenties when I felt bound by geography and graduate school and my deep desire to get married and have a child.

I'm grateful to Ulinich for creating the character of Lena and I'll continue to search for novels that chart the middle of life in new and surprising ways. Elena Ferrante's epic and riveting Neopolitan trilogy comes to mind here, as does Rachel Cusk's still unfolding series which includes *Outline* and *Transit*. I've loved *Wonderland* by Stacey D'Erasmo, *The Folded Clock* by Siri Hustvedt, *Give it to Me* by Ana Castillo, and Jenny Offil's amazing, fragmented novel, *Department of Speculation*. *These writers recognize that in the middle of life, we may experience profound changes. We may feel lost and alone at times, but we don't have to have a mid-life crisis.*

Charting this new middle is about wanting to know who we are separate from the roles our parents and our marriages created for us. Forty-two, for me, is about this hard looking, this sloughing off of roles, staring in the mirror without the acid-induced overlay. I see my ex going through the same struggle, and many of my friends as well. We are trying to forge new relationships that are not built on fear and co-dependence. Now it's about autonomy. The ability to love someone and let them be, and to work hard at messy, improvisational communication.

The new middle is about having your own story—living it and, for me, writing it down. Writing for me, no matter what the genre, has always been a way to manifest difficult feelings, unknown or less-seen landscapes, and people and characters who are messy, absent, or silent.

I don't cook the way I did when I was 21. There are a couple of dishes I make really well that my daughter enjoys—a roast chicken, brownies from scratch, and my mother's strawberry rhubarb pie.

A gluten allergy has recently altered my cooking further, made it more about simplicity and self-care. At 21, I applied a manic energy to most tasks. Cooking and food were performances. Writing was something I did in half-hour jags. I couldn't sustain much else. When my friend poured syrup into my other friend's mouth, she saved her life, but we weren't able to examine then the turbulent push and pull that got us to that moment. We couldn't slow down. We had too much to prove.

I'm busier than ever, but now I cook to save money and feed myself and my daughter healthy food. I'm a good enough cook, and that's okay.

After, I clean up kitchen and sit down to write.

ON SPECTACLE AND SILENCE

The spectacle is not a collection of images; rather, it is a social relationship between people that is mediated by images.

—Guy Debord, *The Society of the Spectacle*

1

We sat on the couch together. I was eight or nine or ten. The burble-voiced sportscasters, the referee's whistle, then, "Personal foul. Unnecessary roughness. Defense. First down." I was, I am, tethered to my father. His fingers twisted a long strand of my hair as we watched. Tight. Tighter still. Release. Repeat. I was there and not there. He used his own hair if I wasn't around, but he preferred mine. It was longer and finer. My father was the one who put my hair in a ponytail before school. He also rebraided my Holly Hobbie doll's yarn hair when it came undone.

We share the same rare neurological condition. It's called Dopa Responsive Dystonia and he and I are the only people I've ever met who have it. I inherited it from him, though he didn't know he had it until a specialist in Toronto finally diagnosed me and I began a successful treatment. Before this small miracle, I was often unable to walk, and falling asleep was a challenge because my muscles were so rigid that they cramped and seized. My father sometimes sat on the edge of my bed and coached me in breathing in and out in an attempt to relax them.

Sometimes we sat in his green Lazy Boy and he read to me from *Winnie the Pooh* and *The Hobbit*. Once, he made me a compartmentalized box out of scraps of cardboard for my rock collection. In the mornings, when I could walk more easily, he took my brother and me to the bird sanctuary. When we arrived at the bird-viewing platform

that overlooked the turtle pond, he took out a Hershey's chocolate bar
and split it into three equal pieces.

2

I scrolled through Twitter to follow the protests in New York City
after the grand jury's decision not to indict Darren Wilson, the Fergu-
son police officer who shot and killed Michael Brown. My kid's dad,
my ex, was there and he sent me pictures from the protest. *FDR shut
down! Manhattan Bridge closed!* I thought a lot that night about the
violence of not being seen or heard and reread some of Darren Wilson's grand jury testimony. Wilson admitted, "And when I grabbed
him, the only way I can describe it is I felt like a five-year-old holding
onto Hulk Hogan. ... The only way I can describe it, it looks like a
demon. That's how angry he looked." Wilson is in a crisis of imagination. This testimony is part of the violence of not being seen or of
misrepresentation. Darren Wilson cannot see Michael Brown. He is
not a person, but an "it."

I thought, too, about the narcissism of this inability to see someone as anything other than an it and the violence of narcissism—of
what happens when we are so wrapped up in our own shit (racist and
otherwise) that we cannot see anyone else.

As I lay on my couch, I wished I were protesting instead of taking
care of my kid, and I remembered the ways I'd moved out of silence
and into protest. The Women's Center on campus freshman year
where we sat in a circle and told our stories. The anti–Gulf War and
pro-choice marches in the early '90s, dipping into and out of Occupy
Wall Street, and more recently at anti-Trump marches. I wondered
then and now about how to be a better ally.

Later that night, I rewatched the video of Officer Daniel Panta-
leo choking and then killing Eric Garner. I saw violence unfolding
in small spaces—the frame of my computer screen and of the cell
phone camera that recorded the video—and the sickening intimacy
of murder, a white man enacting an old wound on a black man. I saw
how violence becomes spectacle and felt the nausea of implication

that my viewing brings with it. Each viewing of the video is, after all, called a hit.

A week later, I took my then six-year-old to Washington Square Park to the protest against police brutality. I tried to frame the protest in a way that made sense to her. She knew about Rosa Parks and often sang a song she learned about her in school, so I started there.

"We're going to a protest."

"What's that?"

"We want to say that something is wrong."

"What's wrong?"

"Well, remember how Rosa Parks protested on the buses, that black people couldn't sit where they wanted?" She nodded. "Well, this is connected."

"How?" she asked. I held up her mittens, in a desperate attempt to get her to wear them. I have been trying to quit nagging because it bores me and doesn't work.

"Well, the police are hurting black people."

"But the police help people. We went to their office. They showed us the jail." She ignored the mittens. She was referring to last year's kindergarten field trip where students learned about "stranger danger" and why police officers carry weapons. She'd come home from the trip scared that she would be kidnapped and with a detailed description of a baton.

"Some help, but some have things they need to work on." I fell back on our shared language for our faults. I was "working on" not being grouchy in the morning. She was "working on" better listening. The police are "working on" not killing innocent black people. I'm not sure this is true. Nuance at six is a challenge.

She shrugged. I dropped the mittens. I wasn't happy with the way I'd framed the conversation, and our time at the protest was brief. We were packed tightly into the space near the fountain and while the chanting was pleasurably loud for me, it was too much for my kid. I couldn't find the meet-up for the other protesters with kids, and so eventually we drifted off to the playground. I wanted her to know that protests happen and that people can and should take to the streets, and I vowed to take her to more protests. When she was three, her dad and I took her to Occupy enough times that, for several months afterward, whenever she saw a police officer in the street, she pointed and said, "Occupy?" This filled us with a twisted lefty glee. Since then, we've taken her to more protests—against police brutality, against the immigration ban, against Donald Trump. I've learned that kids have their own complicated relationships to protesting and that I need to educate her and give her space to make her own signs and speak her own mind.

A couple of weeks after the protest in Washington Square Park I got a Facebook message from an old writing workshop classmate. She'd read one of my essays online and was writing to congratulate me on its publication. Having started a blog about raising more race-conscious children, she was interested in having me write about how I talk to my child about race. I told her I was failing, and she said I could write about that. But when I looked at the blog, I realized that my own language was vague and weird when it came to talking with my child about race and violence, and though I am increasingly comfortable writing about my public failures and humiliations, this one shames me mightily.

3

When I was a freshman in college, a friend and I got caught in the middle of a drunken fistfight between some white sorority girls and some black students. We had been at clubs and bars in the downtown of Binghamton, where we went to school. My friend and I piled into a taxi shuttle back to campus. The details were hazy to me, even the next day, but it began in the casual way that day-to-day racism often unfolds and escalated quickly into violence. A white woman noticed that the black students were sitting in the "back of the bus." She thought this was funny and made a joke about it, as if it were fitting, as if that were where they belonged. The black students objected, and one, a young woman, stood up to protest. Another white woman spat on her. I don't remember who threw the first punch. My friend and I shrank down in our seats. We wanted to disappear. I remember the shame I felt about what the white girls had said, my fear of getting caught in the middle of something, and my decision to say nothing. I remember fists everywhere and covering myself with my arms and wishing it were over. I got punched in the head by one of the black women, and I remember the ringing feel of it. The driver pulled over and threw everyone out of the van. My friend and I scattered and ran through the woods while the fight continued behind us. We went to the campus police. We were asked to make statements, and the campus police officers interviewed us. They filed reports on everyone in the van. At some point, it became clear to us that they wanted to expel the black students. We stopped talking to them because they refused our accounts that the students had been acting in self-defense.

I felt wronged, too. I wanted those young black women to intuit somehow that I was a "good" white person, even though I did nothing to protect them. I believed that such a thing was possible. I suppose I still do—some dreams are harder to let go of than others. Goodness—a good wife, a good mother, a good girl, a good feminist, a good activist, a "good" white person—is deep ideology for me. I have to dismantle it every day.

More than anything, I was disgusted with myself. I was a coward. I tried to protect myself, and I believed I was somehow above the fray. I hid in all of the ways I'd been trained to do as a child, and then I ran away. *Go to your room. Wait for your father. Be quiet. Stay still. Don't move.*

Now I see that punch as the price of my silence. It was an early wake-up call. How can someone know you are on her side if you don't speak up? How can you stand in solidarity if you don't say or do something?

4

His voice in the entryway. Her voice telling him. His feet on the stairs.

We sat on our beds. We were bad. Maybe one of us had lied.

Maybe we'd stolen something. Maybe we'd ripped a hole in the back of the new armchair. Maybe someone else's parents had called about something that had happened at a friend's house. Maybe one of us had left a bike unlocked and it had been stolen. Maybe we'd mouthed off. We did the things that many children do—we broke shit, we made stuff up, we fought and got caught some of the time.

He told us to pull our pants and underwear down. Always. The shame of that exposure. He used a belt usually, and sometimes, if he was really angry, a wooden spoon or the heel of a leather slipper. A hand was not enough for our badness. It lasted as long as it lasted. We couldn't see his face. We heard him breathing hard, felt him winding up, the shock of contact. After, he said things about what we had done and not to do it again. He looked spent. His face was red, his hair out of place.

In the beginning we were punished equally, but when we got older, something shifted. My father stopped hitting me. Maybe to him, I was already a broken body, and so he focused on my brother, who unlike me, had taken to open defiance. I'd learned to keep my transgressions secret and to deny everything. I became a liar. To this day, I can lie on a dime, manufacture a cover story in an instant. It shocks my friends. It's not something I like about myself.

It was summer or winter. Muggy or the dry heat of radiators. I'm not sure. I was in my room with the door open. My brother had been drinking the night before, maybe. I don't know. His door was closed. My parents were fighting about his punishment upstairs. My father wanted to hit my brother, to teach him a lesson, to show him. My mother was against it, said he's too old; in these last years of their marriage she had turned more openly against my father. I heard him on the stairs. He shut my door without looking at me. I got up and listened at the door, but I didn't open it. There was a scuffle in my brother's room, a smaller body being chased by a larger one in a small space, an animal trapped in a cage, desperate to get out. My father yelled and my brother cried and whimpered. There were sounds of contact. That slipper again. Hand against flesh. A scrambling sound.

I didn't do anything. I didn't protect him. As his older sister, shouldn't I have? I was trained in witnessing. Bystanding. A useless silence. It lasted as long as it lasted. My mother came down the stairs. She pushed open the door to my brother's room. She said to my father in an accusing whisper, "Are you done now? Do you feel better?"

5

In the midst of working on this essay, I finally got around to reading Alice Miller's groundbreaking book, *The Drama of the Gifted Child*. I was drawn to it because it's a big part of one of my favorite graphic memoirs, *Are You My Mother?* by Alison Bechdel. It was my ex who gave Miller's book to me. He said that it's a great parenting book and it explained a lot of our struggles with our own parents. We were those gifted children. We were trained to be good and to take care of our parents even as they raged at us and failed us. Our marriage started to fall apart when we both realized we were tired of being caretakers to adults—first our parents and then each other.

I don't know what happened in that room for those muffled couple of minutes because, even though I write from memory nearly every day, memories can be unstable. We called those beatings "spankings" then, but often when I tell close friends about the details, they tell me that it wasn't a spanking. A quick Google search reveals that 84% of Americans believe that sometimes their children need a "good spanking," but I wonder how many of them use household items as weapons (Bazelon). I am inclined to make excuses. I am inclined to call it abuse. It depends on the day. Miller warns, "Sometimes people are convinced that it was just their siblings who suffered humiliation. Only in therapy can they remember—with feelings of rage and helplessness, of anger and indignation—how humiliated and deserted they felt when they themselves were mercilessly beaten by their beloved father" (78). I think I remember all of my beatings, but I am too ashamed to ask my brother about all of his though we regularly text back and forth about my father and begin and end most of these text conversations with "Fuck him." When I can, I have family members fact check my memories. I shared this essay with my brother before its online publication, and though he found it too painful to talk about the details, he told me he was glad I wrote it and gave me permission to publish it.

I wonder how authority gets beaten into our skin at an early age. I believe that our parents make the first marks of the police state on us— their relationship to authority and how they process their own anger gets written onto our bodies. If we are beaten by our parents, will we become docile under the batons of the police later in life or will we become, in turn, violent ourselves? Miller warns, "Oppression and the forcing of submission do not begin in the office, factory, or political party; they begin in the very first weeks of an infant's life" (105).

What is the relationship between domestic violence and racist violence? I keep pulling at this thread. A police state needs some of its officers to be angry victims and willing agents. I do know that our "spankings" made us into shifty, secretive kids and adults with a lot of baggage. Ready witnesses and victims and, on occasion, confused instigators and agents.

6

Maybe it was 1982. I was 10. Jamestown, the dying Rust Belt town in Western New York where I grew up, had one small mall, a low-slung 30-store affair whose centerpiece was Woolworth's. I went to Woolworth's for the pets. I liked to stroke the fur of the guinea pigs, who darted around in a pit of wood shavings. I stared at the jumping puppies and sleepy kittens behind the glass wall. My brother pressed his palms against the python cage and tapped the lizard case until its occupants stepped off their hot rocks.

My love for the Woolworth's pet section was at odds with my hatred of the mall itself. In truth, I was deep in the throes of my then un-diagonosed neurological condition. At six, my pediatrician thought I had cerebral palsy. At nine, a specialist in Buffalo offered up Friedreich's ataxia, a debilitating, life-shortening disorder with no cure. By the time I was ten, all that mattered to me was that by the middle of most days, I couldn't walk. My muscles were rigid—my left hand curled tightly inward; I had to drag my left foot behind me to move forward. The highly buffed concrete floors of the mall were a challenge and to "walk" from Woolworth's to the fountain at the center of the mall took considerable effort and time. People stared. Kids laughed at me. Some of their parents shushed them, but some did not. Sometimes people pointed at me, other times they whispered. I longed to move about unseen or unnoticed, but I often felt like a small-town spectacle, noticeable in my difference—a curiosity, an unknown, a freak.

I've found that small, isolated towns like the one I grew up in encourage staring. Aberrations are especially noticeable, and gossip is a way to pass the time.

"I saw Genevieve coming out of the butcher shop with a big bag."

"I heard on the scanner that she fell off a ladder while changing the light bulb."

There's less staring now when I go home to visit my parents. More people are lost in their cell phones. But even though my disease is treated and not all that visible anymore, I still notice that if I am crossing at an intersection on foot with my daughter, the driver of the car at the light leans forward and stares. My mother says impatiently, "Of course they're staring, they don't know who you are!"

Staring. Spectacle. The voyeur. A looked-at thing.

When my first-year college students are at their grouchiest and most passive, I usually give them an excerpt from Susan Sontag's *Regarding the Pain of Others*. In it, she warns that, while we may feel "obliged" to look at images and photographs of people in pain, we should also consider "what it means to look at them" (95). What Sontag objects to most strongly is our inclination to merely sympathize because this distances us from what we see, and allows us the fiction that we are not involved or implicated. She pleads with us to examine our own privilege in relation to those who suffer and to use that knowledge to take action. My students respond to this text because it remains contemporary, postmodern even, in its understanding of the way we've come to experience so much of what we see. We are far too often passive sympathizers and disinterested consumers. They get it, but they ask why Sontag doesn't tell us how to be active. *What in particular should we do?* I tell them her essay is a form of activism and that their best essays might be, too. They are skeptical about this and I understand why.

7

I had been on Lexapro for three days. I was foggy and nauseous from it, and that combination of symptoms reminded me of my pregnancy. Like then, I was expectant. I wanted to feel better. I wanted less anxiety every day. I wanted not to wake up in the middle of the night panicked and sweaty, and yet I felt the drug was a last resort. My psyche finally won. I was 43; I cried "uncle." My neurologist gave me the prescription eight months earlier, but I took my time filling it. My then-boyfriend was vehemently against it, and I saw, now that we were broken up, that I was very much under his thumb. I was ambivalent but then something shifted. My therapist said, "Why not?" When I started to talk about it with people I know, it seemed a lot of them had tried it or were on it. My neurologist called it "a homeopathic dose." She is the kindest doctor I have ever had, and yet she responds to my anxiety as a purely chemical situation.

And so I tried to write in a very particular fog. First, I was distracted by Karl Ove Knausgaard's essay in the *New York Times Magazine* about driving across parts of the US in search of the Vikings. I was also reading book two of *My Struggle*, and I was in awe of how he makes the everyday, with its parenting failures and shame, a part of his writing. I do not believe his work would be published if he were a woman and an American, but still I love him and he gives me courage. He made me want my fog to be visible to you, and so I named it here. *I am foggy, and still I think and do. I write and I parent and I teach. I wonder how much I can know from this particular drug-addled haze. I am trying to believe in it as I once believed in what I could learn from tripping.*

I was also distracted by poet and essayist Ronaldo Wilson's posts on the Poetry Foundation's *Harriet* blog, "Obliteration Excavations." Ronaldo and I got our MFAs together and we've stayed loosely in touch. I remember him as a benevolent, funny presence in workshops where my work was regularly ripped apart in ways that made me want to hide it from the world. He writes about black bodies, sketching from lynching postcards, about Adrian Piper, Roland Barthes, Mark Wahlberg, Kara Walker, dancing, driving, and a black poetics. I was in awe of him; it's similar to how I felt about Knausgaard, but heightened. Ronaldo and I are peers. I thought I needed to get smarter and read more theory, but it was an old female feeling that I tried to both acknowledge and push away. I've seen Ronaldo dance and read poems out loud and rap, and I knew his essays for *Harriet* have that same movement in them. I believed some of what he's writing connects with parts of what I'm getting at here in this essay, but the Lexapro fog made me too stupid to tease out the thread. I got stuck on this passage about Mark Wahlberg's racism and Kara Walker's "A Subtlety":

> Walker's work enacts a process that fills in the space where I am digging through this old paper, caught in the new realization of Wahlberg's urge for freedom, to be absented from his past, but a past so entrenched with a violent history, that it burns, no matter what he does, no matter what he says, no matter what he wants.

I see Walker and Ronaldo as excavators, artist-historians of particular instances of violence against black bodies, and Wahlberg as the white man who wants to walk away from his violence. I see this essay as my own excavation, a return to my own past violence. Some of us burn more than others in our violent histories, but shouldn't we all excavate and dig?

I've driven in the fog and I've walked through it. The trick is to let go of seeing too far ahead, and isn't that the trick to life, too? I can read the past, but the future isn't even foggy. It's a blank, a vast unknown. I tell myself I like this, but that's a lie.

8

How long does it take to come to a political consciousness? As long as it takes. It's probably too much to claim that a punch propelled me into black history and women's history. Maybe poetry did it, or graduate school, where I began to study the history of feminism and the work of black civil rights activists. Deep friendships with queer folks and people of color have made me see what's at stake in the day-to-day. I've learned how to listen, but I've also had to learn how to speak up. I still struggle to articulate what constitutes a useful silence or when I am merely copping out. In my research for a dissertation about teenage girls who published articles, short stories, essays, and letters in *Seventeen* magazine, I was surprised to find that even this mainstream fashion magazine once had quite a bit of activist writing in it—during the Civil Rights era, *Seventeen* published first-person accounts of life in the segregated south by African-American girls and sent girl reporters to cover national conventions—and that helped me understand that even mainstream capitalist texts are complicated objects and that there are small resistances in even the most repressive spaces. And I remember two books that changed me and taught me how institutional forces shape personal lives—Angela Davis's auto-biography and Simone de Beauvoir's *Memoirs of a Dutiful Daughter*.

I teach a course on activism and the history of youth-led subcultures, but I fail at activism every day. I have too many jobs and a kid and in my free time, I am tired, and still I am trying to fail better at activism by at least being present for it. Attending protests, reading the literature, teaching students about it, telling my story if it matters.

But mostly I teach essay writing, and I've come to believe in the power of storytelling as a vehicle for political change, but only when story moves outward and into history and theory. I teach students to connect their daily struggles to larger political movements, but it is hard work and doesn't have much of a space in academia.

In an essay in the *New Yorker*, "The Long Road to Angela Davis's Library," my friend the poet and essayist Dawn Lundy Martin asks, "Who's to say when the turn from girl to woman happens, or what's in between, in that fold, which one might also call a fount?" From there Dawn proceeds to chart, in her raw and deft way, her own path from Hartford-born, straight, black working-class environmental activist to queer San Francisco–based poet and scholar of black history. Her road to activism opens up a whole new world of texts and conversations. The essay is about the complex ways in which money, race, and power collude to keep people of color and particularly women of color believing they are failures. And yet it's also about Dawn's parents and reseeing her mother as a figure at the center of her struggle for justice. Near the end of the essay, Dawn asks another gripping question:

> What, in the end, is politicization? Is it when you recognize that things are wrong and unjust in the world, or is it when you understand how powerful the powers are that seek to prevent you from changing anything? We learn, over time, that social and political change is made so incrementally that the present can look exactly like the past.

The essay ends with an image of Dawn slipping her mother's hand into her own and the claim that "politicization" is a series of "newly illuminated rooms in the imagination." I am drawn to these images of founts and rooms and to the idea that politicization is in part a reseeing of one's parents and childhood. If knowledge is a house that is constantly under renovation and construction, where do we locate ourselves? In what rooms do I currently reside? Where do I stash my parents, my failures, my shame, or the moments where I got something right and emerged from the fog? This essay, with its multiple sections—each part is a room—functions as the house where I currently reside. I take you from room to room. This is a tour of sorts. We—you and I—are under construction. Perhaps we will renovate this house. Maybe it's just another New York City apartment we will eventually leave behind. We are renters, after all. But we walk around. I point to this wall. You notice a crack. We move to the kitchen to sit down.

During a short visit to New York City, my father told me he'd joined a Facebook group for people with Asperger's syndrome. He sat on my couch while my stepmother and daughter worked on putting together the Lego Cinderella castle he'd brought as a gift.

"How was it?" I asked.

"I had to quit."

"Why? Because you don't have Asperger's syndrome?" I stared over at the hundred-odd Lego castle pieces spread out over the countertop, at my stepmother and daughter bent over the building instructions.

"No," my father sighed. "Those people are a mess. They just complain and complain."

I nodded. Careful in my silence.

"Mama, we can't do the castle without you!" my daughter called out. I walked over to the kitchen, happy for the interruption.

A couple of years ago, in an effort to explain to himself why his relationships with his children were so damaged and why he had so few friends, my father took an online quiz to determine whether or not he had Asperger's. He scored highly though he never followed up with a visit to a neurologist for confirmation. His self-diagnosis gave him an easy way out and followed a trend, particularly among over-achieving men, of autism self-diagnosis. In a recent *New York* magazine article, "Autism Spectrum: Are You On It?," Benjamin Wallace notes that the recent spate of self-diagnosis is often a cover for men who are sadistic or just jerks and who use the label to claim victimhood. *I'm not a bad father. I have a disease. I am not responsible for the relationships I have mangled. I am, ultimately, misunderstood.*

I saw this move toward victimhood as the police turned their backs on Mayor de Blasio during the funeral for the slain Officer Rafael Ramos. I saw it again in a story that a friend, a public middle school math teacher, told me. Two detectives met her outside of her car recently and brought her down to her local police precinct for questioning about her role in the recent protests against police brutality that shut down the Brooklyn Bridge. She told me that one detective tried to explain to her what it was like for police officers during the protests. He said the police felt outnumbered and overwhelmed. He asked her who was watching out for the police. I'm curious about the kind of thinking that erases power realities. I'm wondering how he forgets the police have guns and jails and grenade launchers and tanks at their disposal. I see, too, in these moments that the police don't feel seen or heard, and how easily that can turn into claims of victimhood.

10

When I am feeling open and forgiving, I can see my father as a little boy. The cruelties he suffered at the hands of his own father, who was a colonel in the army, and his mother, who emigrated from Cuba in the early '40s to marry an American 13 years her senior. There's the story of him being tricked into the back of the station wagon full of fiberglass insulation while his father rolled up the windows and cranked the radio to drown out his cries. My father and his brother, who later became a junkie and died homeless in Golden Gate Park, were made to strip naked in the front yard every spring to have their heads shaved. Afterward my grandfather sprayed them with the garden hose and left them to shiver. My father once told me, after I spent the afternoon at my grandma's house practicing Spanish and eating leftover pork chops, *You have no idea what that woman is capable of doing.* I was 16. He described a beating with an electrical cord and how she used her fingernails as a weapon. I remember not believing him. I felt he was trying to poison my relationship with her and keep me from her love, which I badly needed at the time. I can envision my father struggling to walk to school in the hot desert under the Vegas sun. He is sick and no one believes him. His father tells him over and over, *Stop dragging your feet,* and eventually forces him to enroll in the US Naval Academy, where he will be made to stand still for hours and march in lock step. I am not really sure how he survived this. In his first year at the Academy, he will cycle through 14 roommates. He will want to study literature, but his father insists on physics. For years, he'll dream of the life he could have had if he'd become a literature professor and gone to Berkeley. He'll marry my mother, who admits that she cried on her wedding day because she knew she'd made a mistake. They'll stay married for nearly 20 years, even though they often can't stand to be in the same room together. He'll raise two children whom he loves dearly but can't understand. He'll never go to therapy, but he'll construct elaborate theories of the world based on his deep reading. Darwin and Seneca will be his favorites.

ON EATING

1

After I spent the night with a man who was no good for me, I went to the 10:50 a.m. showing of *A Girl Walks Home Alone at Night,* directed by Ana Lily Amirpour. Released in 2014, the film is in Farsi, set in a mythical Iranian town called "Bad City," and was being touted as the first Iranian vampire Western. Into the theater, I brought cheese grits with avocado and chicken meatballs, a brownie frosted with peanut butter, and tea with milk and sugar, purchased from a place I loved, but has since closed, in the Bedford-Stuyvesant section of Brooklyn called Scratch Bread, on the corner of The-Man-Who-is-No-Good-For-Me's street.

I was instantly glamoured. Shot in black and white and containing a love story between a chador-clad vampire woman and a James-Dean-esque son of a junkie, this film is full of sex workers, pimps, and lost souls who wander Bad City's empty, eerily suburban streets. Its star, played by the mesmerizing Sheila Vand and known only as "The Girl," lives in her own subterranean apartment, where she dances to Radio Tehran, Kiosk, and Farah in front of a wall of Madonna and Michael Jackson posters, ticket stubs, and postcards of ruins. Ringing her eyes with black eyeliner, she fastens her chador over jeans and a black and white striped fisherman's shirt and skateboards the empty streets looking for her next victim.

In my favorite scene, she follows a brutal, drug-dealing pimp home and looks on silently as he snorts lines of coke and gyrates to a techno beat. The backdrop of his apartment is pure *Scarface*—glass coffee table, white leather sofa, and mounted trophy heads on the wall. At this point in the film we worry for her because we don't yet know what she is. Will this be the brutal rape of a young woman followed by her initiation into a life of prostitution? Or does she perhaps want him? Will she speak? Her face is blank, pale, and emotionless, and so the answer to any of these questions is hard to tell.

Eventually, The Girl takes his finger into her mouth and sucks on it; her fangs sprout, and she bites it off. As he whimpers for mercy, she pins him down and kills him. The Girl is not our first feminist vampire, but she might be our first Iranian one. She hunts only men and boys, and terrifies a little boy in a frayed suit coat—who is straight out of Italian neorealism, with its child actors and poverty-stricken landscapes—with the warning, "Be a good boy." She swoops in to protect sex workers, and in the shadowy world of Bad City, her chador is more cape than covering, serving not only as a necessity but also a prop.

As I sat in the dark and ate my grits, I thought about women who eat men, the connection between sex and eating, and the way I perhaps use food to compensate for love. I remembered that it was watching *True Blood* at the end of my marriage that made me realize there was something missing in my life—passion and fucking that felt like it was consuming me or I was consuming it.

One of the reasons I returned to the No-Good-Man's house is that he was exceptionally good at eating me out. As the credits rolled, I decided the moment that the vampire begins to kiss and bite its victim's neck is remarkably like the moment when a baby latches onto its mother's breast. Lips to flesh. The fear of being bitten. Suck. Suck.

2

When we were still married, my then-husband and I made an appointment with a person we referred to as the "milk witch." We'd moved to a new neighborhood in Brooklyn, Ditmas Park, that contains an odd stretch of Victorian houses and run-down buildings between the south end of Prospect Park and Midwood. I felt a clash of cultures there—working-class people of color, mostly renters, pushed up against the wealthier white families in the Victorian houses. We were living in one of those run-down buildings and, as usual, I felt I had more in common with the working-class Caribbean women on their way to jobs in hospitals and schools than the rich people in their houses. I'm not sure what those Caribbean women thought of me. Maybe they didn't at all. It was a busy, loud neighborhood on the main drag, full of people who had a lot of shit to get done.

The milk witch was living in one of Victorian houses. She'd been highly recommended by the one of the new moms I knew, who told me that it was typical for lactation consultants to charge $150 an hour. We figured we could afford one session.

At the hospital, I had winced in pain as my daughter tried to latch. It was all bite, no suck. A couple of my friends said the pain would go away, but it didn't. I kept trying. I pumped. We gave her bottles of my breast milk. The nurses in the hospital were too busy to help. Someone came by and lectured me about the importance of breastfeeding and gave me a pamphlet.

The milk witch was kind. I admired her house for its messy family sprawl, her kids in the living room doing their homework—older and alive in a way that I couldn't imagine my baby would ever be. She had me try to feed my daughter and then she weighed her to see if she'd gotten any milk. A little, but not enough.

"Her mouth isn't fully able to latch yet," she said, "so you have to train her. You can't give her the bottle. You'll have to wake up every two hours to feed her. She can do it and so can you." She smiled encouragingly. She told me to buy nipple shields, to come back in a week, and to call her if I had questions.

I woke up every two hours for a week. We tried hard, my daughter and me, her crying red face against my pale, engorged breast. I felt eaten up by what was I trying to do, and yet I got no nourishment from it and neither did she. Soon I was desperate for uninterrupted sleep and prone to hysterical sobbing during the day. The pump felt like a failure, but I used it anyway. My husband gave her bottles so that I could sleep for four hours in a row instead of two. He liked this time they had together in the night and also wanted me to rest.

I knew of other new mothers who were feeding their babies every two hours. They looked tired, but determined. They were not crying in the street. They were breastfeeding in the park and in restaurants under little blankets called "Hooter Hiders." They told me to keep trying and that it would get easier. My husband and my best friend said it was fine if I quit. My mother said it didn't matter as long as my daughter had enough to eat, but it was 2008 and at the height of the "breast-is-best" movement and the media-manufactured "Mommy Wars." Once, a woman I didn't know stopped me on the street to ask me if I was breastfeeding. I stammered out the truth, as if I was on trial, and she seemed smugly pleased about my suffering. I felt ashamed when I bought organic formula and like a failure when I fed my baby from a bottle. There was lot of talk in the air. I remember hearing phrases from successfully breastfeeding moms like, "It's not really a choice for me," and, "If you look at the research, how could you not?

I pumped for five months and supplemented with formula. My daughter never learned how to latch. One day, while I balefully hooked myself up to the pump, my best friend juggled my daughter on her hip and said, "I can't watch it anymore. It's medieval. Please stop."

And so I did.

Like many first-time parents, I wasn't prepared for how all-consuming having a baby would be. I felt fed upon in those early months. Tethered to a tiny mouth and then a machine that was all suck, suck, suck.

3

Recently, my therapist, whom I have been seeing for about four years, asked me to articulate what I wanted in a partner. It's not that this question is new to me, but there was something about it that filled me with a seething rage that made my throat constrict until I managed to yelp, "Don't fucking ask me that question!"

I still struggle with my so-called "transference." I know it's part of the therapeutic relationship, but I have at times thought I was in love with him, and approached our sessions with all of the butterflies and nausea that one associates with third and fourth dates. Lately, I sometimes dislike him, which moves him more from boyfriend to father in my subconscious and is probably an important part of our evolving relationship. He's two years younger than me and when he told me that he was getting married, I burst into hot, jealous tears, and then said, not entirely without meaning it, "Congratulations." I have joked with him that these kinds of moments would do well in an imaginary book I call *The New Yorker Book of Therapy Cartoons*. It's only available during NPR pledge drives and on the sale table at select about-to-fold independent bookstores.

I get, in some stupid, smart-woman way, that in therapy I am re-learning a relationship that was never quite right for me, such as the one I had with my parents; sometimes I am an adult in that room and sometimes I am a little girl. Perhaps I am supposed to learn to voice my desires so that I can believe they are achievable. I don't know. Therapy is confusing.

The truth is, I have actually realized that I have a hard time saying what I want because most of the time I don't believe achieving it is possible, at least in this country, and certainly in my lifetime. But I am challenging myself to say these desires out loud, to protest for them, and to ask for them.

I want affordable housing in okay neighborhoods for lower and middle-income people in cities. I want universities to stop spending all of their money on administrators, new buildings, and tenured faculty, and instead pay adjuncts and contract faculty like myself a living wage— because at places like NYU, where I work full time, and innumerable universities across the country, we now teach well over half of the courses offered to students (Frederickson). I want to stop living in a police state where the shooting of people of color is a daily occurrence and there is rarely justice for the murdered and their families. I want to remember that to protest is my right, and I want to walk the streets without being harassed by the police—who seem to exist only to protect the rich and their property from the nuisance of protesters. I want sex-positive education for all children so that they learn how to speak their desires and know that consent can be hot and not just legal hand-wringing. I want to smash rape culture, so that my daughter can dress however she likes and express her sexuality in whatever way she feels is best for her, among other reasons. I want my students to graduate from college debt-free, politically-empowered, and with a notion of what it means to be a producer and not just a consumer. I want to question ideology in myself and in the systems around me every day. I want essentialist ideas about gender to die while holding on to the right to express all of my girlish ways without anyone questioning me. I want therapy for everyone if they want it and socialized daycare.

Sometimes I want a boyfriend or a partner. Sometimes I fantasize about moving in with this imaginary person. Sometimes he is so handy and industrious that he builds us a cabin in the woods and we live there. Sometimes I buy my own cabin. Sometimes she's a person who likes to dream with me, too. Other times, I sell a novel for half a million dollars and I have enough money to make a down payment on an apartment near Coney Island. Other times, I move to the desert with a bunch of other women friends when we're all in our late fifties, after all of our children have gone to college. But mostly my fantasies involve not living my life in fear, having autonomy, and eventually finding my own permanent place to live.

But I can't say any of this, then, to my therapist in that session. I don't have the language at that moment.

4

In the dark. A different man. Let's call him The-Man-Who-is-Maybe-Good-For-Me. He is a dad. He is something called an Underground Plant Engineer. He looks at maps all day and fixes the cables, tunnels, and wires that bring us the internet. He says this is boring, but I'm riveted. He describes particles of light. Flashes. What's underneath the city and its buildings? There are problems all day. Urgency. We are having a long conversation over three dates. I like him so much that I sing him a song from my childhood about going fishing in a "crawdad hole." I have a terrible singing voice but he likes it anyway. We laugh about my ridiculous rural childhood. We are on my bed. We are kissing. He takes off my pants. He makes jokes about how inappropriate he is, and then he puts his mouth on my pussy and licks and sucks. He uses his finger. He has a beard. Full lips. Bristling. Bracing. I come fast and hard. He keeps his clothes on.

The next day, my friend and I text about a new man in her life, one who is opening her up, helping her see that she has needs of her own and is not wholly independent. She texts me, "But then once you allow yourself to feel them [these needs], where do they end? What if they swallow you whole?"

Love eats us alive: it consumes us and spits us back out again. We eat our loved ones. We lick and suck because it feels good—but aren't we also playing at devouring them? Sex consumes us sometimes, makes us into one moving being. The vampire mimics the kiss so that she can consume. The baby sucks for nourishment. The lover eats us out to open us up.

5

On another occasion, I left the apartment of The-Man-Who-is-No-Good-For-Me at 5:00 a.m. I took a car because it was raining and I'd been up since 3:00 a.m., and even though I was certain I didn't have enough money to make it to the end of the month, I didn't care. Before I left, I took the package of Ho Hos we bought the night before at the deli and put them in my bag, and I wrote him a note: "*Dear Wolf. Insomnia made me miss my bed, so I took a car home. All safe. Hope I didn't wake you. Will text later. Your Red.*"

This was a game we played. Little Red? Riding Hood and the Wolf. We played it more when we were in a monogamous relationship. It was a narrative we liked because it was simple. He was a large bearded wolf in the forest. I was a lost red-haired girl. Sometimes there was a woodsman who was looking for me. Sometimes I was innocent, and sometimes I tempted him. He found me. He bit me. He took me. A fairy tale. A porn fantasy. It worked surprisingly well.

In the car ride home, I stared out the back seat window at the Brooklyn lights—streetlights, streetlamps, brake lights, deli signs, and bar neon. The city is a string of lights that glamours me. *I'm here for the lights*, I wanted to say, because it's one of the few things left in the city that still dazzles me.

My insomnia upset me. Not because I didn't know its contours, but because I'd been on Lexapro for the last months and for the first time in almost five years, I was sleeping through the night. I had decided I was no longer an insomniac, yet I woke up thinking about The-Man-Who-is-Maybe-Good-For-Me, whom I was seeing the following night. I missed him, which bothered me because I just met him. He sent me his picture before I fell asleep next to The-Man-Who-is-No-Good-For-Me.

I woke up thinking about a poem to write, the student essays I must comment on, my friend's new YA manuscript I am reading, and whether or not the H&M coupon on my counter has expired. I wondered if it c possible for me to love two men at the same time. I thought of my friends in open relationships and the Dear Sugar podcast featuring my freshman year roommate and fellow poet, mom, and friend, Arielle Greenberg, who lives with both her husband and her boyfriend. I thought she is brave and I am confused. I worried I didn't have enough time and that these men were neither good nor bad, just these interesting men I knew, and that it was simply easier to cast them in role of the low-down and no-good and the promising and maybe-better because I didn't know what I wanted. I woke up, like I used to wake up before Lexapro. Panicked. Manic. The usual.

When I got home, I opened the computer. I boiled water for instant coffee and I arranged two of the three Ho Hos on a plate. I added half an avocado from the refrigerator in an attempt to make it a healthier breakfast. I wrote and I ate the first two Ho Hos. They were sweeter than I remembered from my childhood, and then I ate the third one, too.

6

In one of my favorite scenes from the movie *Wild*, based on the best-selling memoir by Cheryl Strayed, Reese Witherspoon, who plays the young Strayed, eats her mother's ashes after she has died from cancer.

Gray smudge on pink lips. The daughter on the ground. Hungry. Grieving. A primal ingesting, a way to eat the mother and to bring her back into a living body.

When an interviewer asked Strayed if she'd really done this, she said, "Yes. My family and I had spread my mother's ashes in this plot of land that I grew up on in northern Minnesota, and there was just this little bit left, and I could not let go of my mother in the material world. I couldn't do it, so I did what came naturally to me, and so many people have written to me to say, 'I did that too.'"

The womb. The breast. The mother's body. Ingest. Ingest.

Lately, my daughter has taken to resting her hand on my breast and saying, "I'm going to touch your boob for a little while." I wonder if this is an unconscious desire on her part to reclaim the breast. Or maybe breasts just feel nice. My ex told me she's been doing it to him, too, usually while they're watching cartoons together. More tether. More touch. *I come from you, and though we are separate now, I will claim you even from this small distance.*

When I first started seeing my therapist, I longed for him to hug me. It felt like a primal ache, something prehistoric in my bones. Maybe it was the baby I once was and her desperate desire to be picked up and held for as long as she wanted. I had colic and a hernia, all in my first year. According to my mother, I could not be held enough. *You didn't want anyone but me.*

In her beautiful graphic memoir, *Are You My Mother?*, Alison Bechdel, examines her complicated relationship to her mother and remembers the moment her first therapist, Jocelyn, hugged her. The hug happens after Bechdel cries freely for the first time in a session. A year later, Bechdel finds herself wanting another hug, and this time, Jocelyn won't do it. Bechdel, who is also writing about the psychoanalyst D.W. Winnicott writes:

> Winnicott enumerates the "unthinkable anxieties" of the newborn. 1. Going to pieces. 2. Falling forever. 3. Having no relationship to the body. 4. Having no orientation. The good-enough mother staves these off by literally holding the baby together. The analyst also provides a holding environment for the patient…but this means the analyst's attention, the physical room, the couch. (272)

Why won't Bechdel's therapist hug her a second time? We never quite know, but Bechdel realizes that a second hug from Jocelyn, in the midst of her unraveling relationship with her girlfriend, "would have been to drop me analytically" (273). Love, whether it's romantic, familial, or therapeutic is about the hug, but the therapist walks a fine line. They hold us in the space of the room so that we feel "hugged enough," but mostly they can't touch us.

Skin against skin. Contact. Flesh. I see you because I hold you. I keep holding you until I let you go.

My favorite yoga teacher, Rebecca, adjusts my shoulders when I'm in warrior two and presses down on my lower back during child's pose. Most days I am hungry for this touch. She's the only teacher who has ever convinced me to invert. She held my legs in place, as my stomach muscles quivered. Afterwards, she rubbed my neck as a I cried tears of joy.

My therapist has never hugged me. I haven't asked though I've wanted to. Once, when he left the room in the middle of one of our first sessions to use the bathroom, I sniffed his jacket, which was hanging on the back of the door. It was an animal impulse. Smell has always been powerful for me—I like armpits and flowers equally. I confessed, in deep shame, a couple of sessions later, but like most good therapists, he rolled with it. "You're getting to know me," he said. "You want to make sure that I exist."

More recently, when I'm angry with my therapist, I tell him our relationship doesn't matter because it doesn't exist outside of the room where we meet. "No," he insists, "We're here together and this is real."

7

One of my high school best friends gave birth to twin girls. She was already a mother of two, so this makes four kids in all, and though we have not seen each other since our early twenties, I keep track of her loosely on Facebook. She's a breastfeeding activist and home schools her kids, and I'm both overwhelmed by her life and excited by all that she manages. She was breastfeeding the twins and, according to my

Facebook feed, it was going well (breastfeeding twins while reading a Kindle!), although she did post that she wishes men could lactate, too, so her husband could take over.

I dreamed recently that I went to visit her in the upstate New York town where she lives. I walked into her house, took off my shirt and bra, sat down in her nursing chair, put a twin on each breast, and fed them. My friend looked on for a minute and then padded off to take a shower. I felt some surprise that I still had milk, but I did. The babies latched and sucked and there was no pain.

I'm sure there are less obvious ways to read this dream, but for me it was a reunion on many levels. I was initially to give birth to twins, but I lost one in the fourth month of my pregnancy, and so, in this dream, I held the twin I never met and I fed them both in the way I thought I might in those first early months of my pregnancy. In the dream, my old friend was very much the girl I remember, with beautiful red hair and small, perfect feet. But a mother of four now! Like all high school friendships, ours was intense and romantic. I felt she was trapped in her home, and so I dreamed of rescuing her, but I see now that it was probably me that longed to escape my own breaking home.

I reunited with the mother inside of me who wanted to do everything right and who still thought that was possible. The mother is a fantasy mother, and I suspect she, or the idea of her, lives in all of us. She's perfect and ready because nature made her that way. She doesn't need a lactation consultant or a bunch of books, and certainly not Lexapro. She's good to go, right out of the gate.

Perhaps my dream was a sort of goodbye to this fantasy mother. I'd like to think it could be that easy.

8

I asked The-Man-Who-is-No-Good-For-Me to read this essay because I felt stuck. He said that there are two essays here: one about breastfeeding and eating, and one about dating and my therapist. I sat with that for a week and decided he was wrong, so I persisted in tying these threads together, these pieces and parts. I feel it's the essayist's job to put seemingly contradictory evidence in conversation. Or perhaps I am the feminist who delights in making you think about fucking, eating, and breastfeeding all in one place.

Women's bodies, more so than men's, are dual landscapes—they can be for nourishment and for sex. The breast is the site for that overlap. Babies suck it, but so do lovers. We all need to eat.

In another essay in this collection, I called OkCupid the "man store," but I realize that it's more complicated than that. It's like a menu with pictures and elaborate descriptions for food that will most likely never arrive because there are too many choices, and as a guy I was recently dating—whom I did not meet on OkCupid—said, "OkCupid makes everyone crazy." Maybe he was right.

Psychologists who study choice have determined that, contrary to what we've been led to believe by marketing departments, too many choices actually exhaust us and leave us feeling unfulfilled.

Sometimes OkCupid can feel like a vista of possibility, but mostly, it's a huge time suck. The-Man-Who-is-No-Good-For-Me says it's best to treat it like a weird video game, and dating as an anthropological adventure. He's always been more positive than me.

Scrolling through pictures of men and sometimes women reminds me of why I periodically take Facebook off my phone. I want to avoid the late night, boredom-induced nothingness that feels like the nadir of late capitalism. All screen. All voyeur.

No face. No contact.

And still sometimes I go on dates: first dates that don't involve food, but just drinks because the date is the food, the person you may or may not want to taste, to see again, to get to know better.

The one who was a DJ and a concert promoter and unemployed and angry.

The one who was a bartender in Red Hook with a beard and a bench press in his bedroom.

The one with three kids who didn't really have time to date.

The one from before.

The one from Rome who writes film reviews for an Italian website and has Dennis Rodman's jersey number tattooed on his forearm.

The one who protests rent hikes and anti-rent-stabilization initiatives.

The one who likes pottery and utopian communes.

The one Who-is-No-Good-For-Me. The Wolf.

The one Who-is-Maybe-Good-For-Me.

The one who says he lives in New York but really lives in Baltimore.

The one who broke his ankle and is still living with his ex.

I'd like to think that in fifty years we (or our children) will look back and laugh at the folly of sites like Facebook and OkCupid. Or maybe we'll have fully moved into what Maureen O'Connor in her *New York Magazine* article calls "The Voltron Theory of Casual Dating," which is based on the 1980s cartoon, *Voltron: Defender of the Universe*, in which several smaller robots join to form one super robot. O'Connor writes:

In the absence of one good partner, an actively dating single person will naturally construct a corpus of complementary partners who, if assembled into one giant Voltron partner, would be his or her ideal boyfriend or girlfriend. (Much like the Wu-Tang Clan.) Occasionally, the Voltron becomes so attractive that it eclipses the appeal of any one person. This shift marks either the downfall of dating, or the beautiful escape from infuriating gender roles and frustrating pressures to nail down a spouse.

I see myself sliding towards the Voltron theory, and it's okay, fun, and even good at times. But I wonder if unlimited choice is making me unable to commit—or am I just moving away from the goal-oriented model of dating? Am I eating all of the cake? What if I just love a lot of cake?

9

Sometimes my ex and I get together with our kid to have family time. We worry that she misses the two-parent experience now that she travels back and forth between us. On a recent Sunday morning, I took the train to the Bedford-Stuyvesant section of Brooklyn where he just moved. They were deep into a game called "Bakery," which I quickly joined. They had drawn cookies, cakes, baguettes, cupcakes, candy, and croissants and arranged them on a chair. My ex and I were put to work either as customers or sous-chefs while our daughter ran the bakery she'd named Zally's. I was especially adept at playing customer—voicing some faux-anxiety about guests arriving soon and having nothing to feed them, buying up al the baked goods with pretend money and then noisily gobbling what I'd bought just outside of the store.

It turns out that fake baked goods give me just as much pleasure as real ones and parents who binge on fake food are funny. Six-year-olds, not surprisingly, like to be in charge of the food, and I am a glutton even when I play.

10

I re-watched *A Girl Walks Home Alone at Night* once it started streaming on Netflix, and, though I still loved its black and white beauty and startling imagery, I noticed the second time around that it's essentially a moral story. The bad men are ultimately punished, and the woman vampire drives off into the darkness with the one good man in the movie: Arash, the son of a junkie. I came to realize that most stories about terrifying, out of control, or grieving women are made safe in the end by the promise of a monogamous relationship. The man heals the woman and makes her safe again. Cheryl Strayed's journey in *Wild* is comforting because, at the end of her long walk alone on the Pacific Crest Trail, standing on Bridge of the Gods outside of Portland, she forecasts her future: a husband and two children. Her journey alone is coming to an end! She won't die a withered, old, grouchy hag! Though I love this book, I'm more interested lately in stories about women that do not wrap up neatly, do not end in marriage, and do not make the woman safe because she is coupled.

11

On some nights I am a woman who walks home alone. Not a girl, though I see myself as girlish still—running in ankle boots, blushing around certain tall men, and playing pretend with my daughter.

I recognize that I had to let that girl go. She had ideas about marriage and men, breastfeeding and babies, ideas that I now know were fantasies.

It's a second date, this time with a father of two teenage boys. We smoke a cigarette through the screen of my window and drink whiskey. I attempt to do a four-card Tarot reading for him, but I'm still learning the Tarot, and I have to use my friend and poet, Hoa Nguyen's, handouts. He draws the Queen of Cups for his present card. In my mythic deck, she is Helen of Troy, a woman whose beauty was so great she started the Trojan War. I read out loud to him from Hoa's notes: "Deep love, untapped feeling, deep self-knowledge, and super sexy!"

He takes off my clothes on the narrow couch. His lips press on top of mine. Against my neck and then breasts.

I want in this moment to be eaten up. Devoured.

Later, I'll want to do the eating. I won't know the table or the restaurant. I don't even think I'll know how to get there, but I hope I'll know when I'm full.

THE BLOODY SHOW

1

Like many a lady nerd, I was deep into Elena Ferrante's Neapolitan trilogy. When the fourth and final installment of the series came out, I went to a book party at a Brooklyn bookstore to celebrate. The large back room was packed with women of all ages—mostly white, some in cute glasses and sun dresses, shod in low-heeled sandals, Birkenstocks, and the occasional cute lace-up Oxford. There weren't many men there: a couple of reliably bearded types and the flustered twenty-five-year-old who was in charge of the cash register and looked like he might faint from all of the overly kind requests to buy the *The Story of the Lost Child*.

I bought two copies—one for me and one for my friend who was running late from the airport—and bolted. I couldn't quite take the energy in the room. It was a party without its star because Ferrante lives in Italy and is famous for not making appearances. No fan has ever met her, and I'm pretty sure I would throw up if I did. It was hot in there and I couldn't move. We were waiting for a panel of other writers to talk about Ferrante. I didn't want to talk about her. The third book had ended with a cliffhanger. I finished it two weeks before, and I'd been wandering around since, desperate to know what had happened to Elena (Lenu), the protagonist and narrator.

At a nearby bar, I ordered a beer, cracked the spine, and started reading. I didn't even check to see if there was anybody cute sitting next to me.

It's hard to explain the effect of this series. I've had conversations with other readers, mostly super articulate women writers, about Ferrante. Reading her has altered us. We've stayed up all night and ignored children, partners, and lovers. Work obligations have slid to the side.

"At eight o'clock, my kids were like, are you ever going to make dinner?" my friend, a poet and academic, told me.

"I'm not going out," another friend said to me. She's a single mom, also a poet, and this was the one night during the week that she could see her boyfriend. "I just want to read Book Four."

I ignored my daughter in the bath as I read on the couch for an hour until

She emerged with pruney fingers and toes and said, "Don't you want to wash my hair?" "Oh, next time," I said, barely looking up from Book Three.

This is fitting because the book is partially about the pull between domesticity and a creative life. It charts a decades-long friendship set largely in Naples, Italy, between two poor girls—Lenu, who leaves to become a famous writer, and Lila, her clever best friend who stays. The book follows Italian politics, feminism in Italy, student uprisings, marriages, deaths, murders, funerals, births, and affairs. What I love most about the series is how emotional it is. There is no feeling that Ferrante won't explore and many of them are still taboo. Female jealousy. Sexual passion. Rage. Bad choices and the ways that we defend them. Mother-love that is full of both devotion and hate. How we sometimes choose lovers over children. The ways women still suffer for love and give up so much of ourselves to have it, in spite of how smart we are and how much we've read.

In a way, reading Ferrante has turned me into the kind of mother I grew up with. My mom didn't play with us that much. She had her own life. She was on the phone or cooking or reading or at work and we were to amuse ourselves. That's how it used to be in the 70s.

Buying the book and leaving like a fugitive to be alone with it reminded me of the masturbatory experience I used to have when I was a teenager: ordering an independent cassette from the local record store/arcade/drug den where I spent every day after school, hanging on the wing of the video game Galaga while some skater punk boy I was obsessed with tried to reach high score. I only left when one of my cassettes had come in from England or from the magical land of Sub Pop Records. I remember palming the Cocteau Twins *Blue Bell Knoll* and running out of the store to catch the bus so that I could get to my room, lock the door, and listen. When The Smiths *The Queen is Dead* arrived, I grabbed my best friend's hand and we walked slowly to her apartment imagining out loud what Morrissey would have to say, ignoring her Italian mother's plea that we please eat something when we came through the door, and then lying on the floor of her bedroom to listen.

Art could break my teenage-boy-watching spell, could turn me from passive little worm into a girl who made choices, had passions, and could leave at any time.

Later, when I started to have sex with boys, I'd learn that you could both listen to a new album and fuck, thereby doubling the pleasure. In college, entire relationships were sustained on the back of an album. Patti Smith's *Horses*. Joni Mitchell's *Blue*. A Tribe Called Quest's *The Low End Theory*.

I still have that sensation when I'm on the train and my kid has just gone to her dad's and I feel free in a way that is still new to me—still teenage, actually. It's usually Miley Cyrus, Nicki Minaj, or Rihanna who makes me giddy. "We Can't Stop" and "I'm Feeling Myself" and the hilarious "Bitch Better Have My Money," which really should be the soundtrack for freelancers and teachers everywhere.

To have the time to get lost in a book. In a whole album. In just one song. To ignore the world. To pulse with it.

2

"Wait, ask me if you can fuck me?" I said to him. I called this man, whom I'd been in a monogamous relationship with for a year and then an open one for the last six months, "The Man Who is No Good For Me." Lately, I wasn't sure what to call him. My best friend. My muse. I didn't know, but we were trying something new. Not fucking. Me not fucking anyone. For a little while. As a reset. As a curative. For rest.

We sat at the bar of an Italian restaurant in the West Village. I was hungover from a date with a stranger the previous night. I kissed the date on a park bench while a gaggle of teenage boys skated by. "Must be nice!" they called to us. The date walked me to the mouth of the subway and said goodbye. When I got home, I couldn't sleep. Too much whiskey. Empty post-first date feeling. I haven't seen him since.

I had PMS, too. I knew it because I got teary on the walk to the restaurant because my neighborhood felt unbearably WASPy and stupid—full of bankers, women in short white dresses, and gay men carrying bags that were either meant to look like a workman's tool kit or were a workman's tool kit.

We'd just finished an heirloom tomato salad and were waiting for our pasta. Later, he'd go on a date with another woman and I'd wander into the Cubby Hole, a lesbian bar, and then chicken out and walk home.

"Will you fuck me?" he asked, playing along.

"I'm so sorry. I can't," I said in mock sorrow. "I'm on a dick break," and then I mimed looking at a fake watch on my wrist. We both laughed.

3

I'm not sure when I started to believe that a man could solve all my problems, but I do remember when I first decided that not having a boyfriend or even boys who liked you was the worst possible thing that could happen to a girl. It was the ninth grade, the first year of high school and probably the most miserable year of my teenage life. I'd gone from a smallish middle school of 200 kids, where I had a best friend who was a boy and several other best friends who were girls, to a gigantic 1000-plus kids high school. Because of the indifferent cruelties of scheduling, I wound up separated from all of my middle school friends. I did not have a single class or even lunch with Denis or Cynthia or Erica. I was on my own, and I felt it so acutely that I started eating my lunch in a bathroom stall so that I wouldn't have to face the cafeteria alone. I came to enjoy these fifteen minutes of solitude where I ate a soggy piece of pizza with my feet up on the walls of the stall and my butt over the lidless toilet. Once I snuck past the cafeteria monitors, I was home free. Friendless, but free.

My high school had a tradition on Valentine's Day. Maybe it raised money for charity, I don't know. In retrospect, it seemed designed to humiliate and shame in that '80s way that inspired so many John Hughes movies. For a dollar, you could send a carnation to anyone, and during homeroom, the cheerleaders or the student council or whoever ran the sale delivered the flowers. I remember they could be purchased anonymously or you could sign your name. Some girls—I remember one of the most popular ninth grade girls in our school, a petite cheerleader with an amazing rack and a throaty voice, got an armload of flowers, a Miss America-like bouquet, that made her look both proud and overwhelmed. I hated her, but that wasn't new. Because of the alphabet, I sat behind her in many classes. Mostly, she ignored me unless she wanted something. An answer on the math quiz. The homework from English. She wasn't mean to me, but she couldn't seem to ever quite rest her eyes on me. It pained her to say my name. I felt like a piece of furniture to her—invisible until she needed a place to put a glass or sit down. I watched boys flirt with her. I saw her pass notes. I was wildly jealous.

Other girls got one or two or three. Another had a dozen. A couple of us had none.

The sting was intense. I'd already had a shitty, friendless year and this confirmed it. The girls who got a couple flowers were smart enough to send them to one another, to pay it forward. Not only did I feel incredibly unloved at the time the flowers were distributed, but there was also the spectacle of the whole rest of the day. Watching other girls in the hallway carry around their flowers—in bundles, on top of their book piles, shoved into their backpacks and purses. Ah, the luxury of being given so many flowers that you were actually annoyed! Those of us without flowers were marked. Unloved. Unwanted. Invisible. Or at least that's how I read the whole thing through my teary ninth-grade eyes.

4

On the same day that I deactivated my OkCupid account, I also bought a DivaCup. If you're unfamiliar with a DivaCup, please go buy one right now. It's basically a little latex cup that fits nicely and imperceptibly in your vagina to collect your period blood. Excited? You should be! Because now you don't have to spend twenty bucks every month on chemical-filled paper products that will destroy your body and the earth with harsh dyes and excess paper waste!

Anyway, it was a shitty day. My daughter was on a vacation with her dad for nine whole days and I was missing her. I'd just returned from a two-day visit with my friend out on Long Island, and I was feeling the return to solitude acutely. I had therapy. I was on a dick break. The semester was starting in less than two weeks and I was woefully unprepared. I shut down my OkCupid account as a final gesture of "Uncle." I was sick of writing to guys who never wrote back to me and fielding messages that were illegible or prematurely graphic. I was never a prude on that site, and from time to time, I was game for some dirty talk with a stranger, but there was too much of it lately. I'd been on a bad date with a guy who insisted on paying for a fancy dinner and then told me I'd earned it. I was annoyed by a first message that read, "Do you have experience with BDSM?" Could we maybe slow it down a little? And I felt wholly incensed when a toothless man (I mean, two front teeth just gone, as if he were my seven-year-old and was waiting for the tooth fairy to show up) asked me out. "Teeth!" I texted my muse, "are a basic fucking requirement for dating in New York City!" I grew up with my share of toothless upstate New Yorkers. I just couldn't.

The DivaCup is a bit tricky at first. It sits low in your vagina, not high like a tampon. And so I spent a lot of that day feeling around in there, trying to get the whole thing, well, situated. The truth is, I hadn't had my hands in my vagina in a while, and it felt nice. It also reminded me how amazing vaginas are—all the things they can hold. Tampons! Little silicon cups! Dicks! Dildos! Babies! The DivaCup instructions come with some nice reminders about vaginas. They say,

"The vagina is an elastic, muscular tube only about 3–4 inches (8–10 centimetres) long." After you get the cup positioned the right way, you have to turn it 360 degrees to get the cup to open up and suction to your vagina. I couldn't get the trick of it at first, but when I did, it was like, *voilà*! Magical suction! The vagina just grabs on and holds it. I imagined this must be what it's like to put your dick in a vagina. Held. Warm. Tight. Ahhh.

I remembered that I started wanting to use tampons in the ninth grade, in that same shitty year. I'd been wearing bulky pads and I found them bunchy and uncomfortable. It was the time of the original high-waisted acid wash mom jeans. Shut up twenty-something women of Bushwick and Williamsburg! You have no idea how uncomfortable the original version of those jeans felt. They were tight and the fabric was too thick and they had no stretch and we were all determined to wear them. Tampons, according to everybody cool and *Seventeen* magazine, were a fashion requirement. It took me until tenth grade, when a guy fingered me and broke my hymen—I think I may have used him for that very purpose—to figure out the whole tampon thing. Ever since I realized I could put things in my vagina, I have wanted to—tampons, sure, fingers, yes, dicks, please.

I have used sex to disassociate from my life, as a salve for wounds I couldn't name, to claim power, and to stop thought.

5

In the newest best-friend version of our relationship, my muse and I are going to the movies and eating a lot. Perhaps we should just get married and call it a day.

We saw *Diary of a Teenage Girl*, which is based on the graphic novel of the same name by Phoebe Gloeckner. I read the book long ago, taught it for a semester or two in my *Teenager in American Culture* course, and even managed to get Gloeckner to come out and headline a zine conference my students and I cooked up. Gloeckner was lovely to us and beautiful in a way that I think stunned us all into silence. We were comic book nerds after all. I remember an awkward dinner. I remember that I was in awe of her and that I couldn't really speak because I wanted to write a novel, but at the time I didn't know how.

The movie, which is set in San Francisco in 1976 and is about a fifteen-year-old girl, Minnie, who loses her virginity to and has an affair with the boyfriend (Alexander Skarsgård) of her single, swinging mom (Kristen Wiig), made us both cry. Bel Powley plays Minnie perfectly. Gloeckner, Powley, and the director of the film, Marielle Heller, get that Minnie is both simultaneously a child and a totally sexual being who is in full control of what she's doing. What I'd forgotten that I loved so much about the book, and that is also totally present in the movie, is Minnie's sexuality—the way she'll do anything for Monroe, how badly she wants him, in spite of her mother, regardless of any of it. She is, at this stage in her life, all about that particular dick. She and her friend Kimmie blow strangers in a bar bathroom, and Minnie is interested in girls, too, but she follows Monroe wherever he allows her to go—his car, his apartment, and the couch in her mother's house. No matter that this longing is destructive and dangerous, Minnie is unstoppable. I suppose they could have picked a slightly less attractive actor to play Monroe. I remember the book made me feel more creeped out by their affair. Monroe seemed a bit uglier, hairier, and more manly while Minnie seemed a little more girlish. But I've never recovered from my then-married lady crush on Eric in the first two seasons of *True Blood*, so I am happy to see him here doing, well, anybody.

At the end of the movie, fresh from her break-up with Monroe after her mother finds out what has happened and a rough couple of weeks where Minnie runs away and hooks up with a lesbian drug addict, Minnie says: "This is for all the girls who have grown," and in comparing herself to her mother, who she believes needs a man to be happy, she continues, "What if nobody loves me? What if that's not what it's about?"

And it was those last three lines that really made me cry, because Minnie gets something at fifteen that I'm still struggling with at forty-three: *So what if I am unloved? Isn't there so much else for me to do here on this planet? Can't I let this go?*

Well, yes and no.

6

You see, Minnie is actually more powerful than Monroe. When they take acid together, Minnie grows wings and floats above the bed, happy and free. Monroe sobs in a heap on the floor about how much he loves and needs her. In one of the last scenes of the movie, after Minnie's mom finds out about their affair, Monroe is out of their lives, and Minnie and her mother have made up, Minnie sells her drawings on the boardwalk and Monroe jogs by. She gives him one. He looks freaked out. He's a vitamin salesman. They shake hands. That's it.

I think the skewed power is why some younger women are attracted to older men. I know that was the case for me. When I was nineteen, I fell in love with a guitarist in a semi-famous indie band from my hometown. He was thirty-three. He had money and fame and a house with furniture in it and unlimited pot and I had just been dumped and after some squeamishness on my part about his body, I was totally all in. But the thing was, I always felt that I was the more mature one, the one who was going somewhere and who was definitely smarter than he was. It was partially youthful arrogance and, eventually, sadly true. He died of liver failure at forty-two, after we'd lost touch for several years. The funeral was closed casket. There was a lot of gossip in the parking lot about drug overdoses and gay lovers. I left the funeral crying and confused.

Minnie will make it because she's an artist. She can draw her way out of anything. She can put that blood on the page, stare at it, and publish it. I found this comforting. A reminder for all of us about how to be whole. Make shit. Be a producer.

7

Never mind what I said about the DivaCup. After two days of trying to get it to sit comfortably in my vagina without hurting me when

I walked, I gave up and returned to tampons. I was disappointed. I wanted to save money and the environment with my forward-thinking menstruation practices! I failed. I texted my friend, "I think I have a crooked vagina." She texted back, "Aren't all vaginas crooked?"

That same friend sent me an article from *Vanity Fair*, "Tinder and the Dawn of the 'Dating Apocalypse,'" by Nancy Jo Sales, and I got caught up in the stories from twenty-something investment bankers and sorority sisters about how Tinder is turning dating into a video game. Sales argues that while this new app has made it easier to find dates, these dates are woefully unsatisfying and the app has turned men into a bunch of "fuckboys." I sent it to my muse who reminded me that Nancy Jo Sales is sometimes a fear-monger, and the next morning, I woke up early and found Jesse Singal's, "Has Tinder Really Sparked a Dating Apocalypse?" The answer is, not surprisingly, no. Sales, according to Singal, ignored data from researchers showing that millennials are actually having less sex than Generation Xers. Sales also doesn't interview anyone who has had a positive experience on OkCupid or Tinder. I know a few.

At the time, I wasn't on Tinder. I was wary of the swipe right if you like someone, swipe left if you don't format. I liked the longer profiles on OkCupid which told me a lot about the person. My experiences on OkCupid are mixed, but they are probably better than what I would have done in a bar or through friend set-ups like we used to have to do in the '90s. I met the muse, whom I fell in love with and then we broke up and then we got back together and, well, I don't know. But no matter what, he's a pretty good friend. I met a couple of scary guys—the over-medicated one who stared too much at my face, the sad unemployed guy who wouldn't stop texting me for a month—and I've met guys who don't really have time to date because of their crazy jobs and their responsibilities to their exes and their kids. The dads of OkCupid—and I'm speaking of the three or four I've dated—are doing too much, frankly. They are mostly still supporting their exes (through alimony or mortgage payments or health insurance) who have not managed to find full-time work, and they are seeing their children whenever they can (mostly weekends and one night a week), and they are working very demanding jobs and they are exercising. They think they have time to date, but they don't. So although I'm very drawn to the idea of dating a dad, I think if I go back to OkCupid, I'll stick with non-dads. They just have more time. If anything, I think capitalism—trying to make it in America—is what makes dating impossible. Everyone is too busy trying to survive in New York to truly take the time to get to know someone and fall in love. It's no surprise that the investment bankers in their twenties that Sales spoke to treat dating like the stock market. Volume. Margin. Yield.

Honestly, the main reason I miss being in a family unit is the illusion of financial security I used to have. I no longer have a husband to save me or take care of me. I never really had that anyway, but the idea of it was comforting.

8

In my favorite sketch from the show *Portlandia*, "Put a Bird on It," Fred Armisen and Carrie Brownstein play a hipster couple who transform a home décor boutique by putting stencils of birds on everything. The sketch reaches a kind of fever pitch of birding—on tote bags, lamps, t-shirts, and pillows—until real birds fly into the store and destroy everything. The bird is the cure-all to the ennui of late capitalism. It makes the silly object somehow more natural and the twee a little less cloying. The sketch also effectively broke my desire for anything ever with a bird on it, which is a good thing for a middle-aged woman who is drawn to artisanal pickles, stenciled pillows, and Mary Jane shoes. Still, the sketch is really about our desire to put something good on top of anything bad to make it tolerable.

Like those silly hipsters who put birds on shit, I have long put dicks on top of problems to make them go away or to lessen the pain they cause me. Bad teaching day? Put a dick on it! Feel like a failure as a writer? Put a dick on that! Horrible, boring, bad-mom feeling. Dicks will help! I have used dicks for comfort, solace, loneliness, and anger. Orgasms are calming. They release endorphins. Dicks can help with orgasms. Of course, many of these dicks were attached to men I love, but some were just dicks.

So, what is a dick break, then? I suppose it is a time for actually feeling the boredom, pain, loneliness, and anger. Sigh. When I was in group therapy, I admired the men who said they felt nothing, who were comfortably numb. Feelings are hard. They hurt. I've always had way too many of them. Remember ninth grade? Ugh. I'm still writing about it. Maybe that's why I love working with teenagers and was so obsessed with the characters in Ferante's trilogy that I sometimes thought they were real. My students and Lenu and Lila feel a lot. Feeling is the plot of their lives, hurling them forward into space and time, and that's always made sense to me.

9

A week into the dick break, I bought *The Small Backs of Children* by Lidia Yuknavitch and read it in a night. The cover is red with the black outline of a girl's body falling. The book is about an American woman writer who becomes obsessed with an Eastern European girl she sees in a photograph. This photo of a girl emerging out of the bomb wreckage that kills her entire family is what sets the story in motion.

The sex scenes in this book are powerful and primal. Real, hot, and a little bit scary. They remind me of the way sex and art can exist outside of commerce.

We insist on our own tiny productions—fucking, shitting, and coming. We love the traffic and noise of it because we are underground animals. We need small moments when we refuse to be upright, good consumers. These acts go nowhere and yet they matter. Pure pleasure and absolute release.

Sometimes sex is the thing we do best. Our most animal selves. Often cum, shit, and blood are all we can leave behind.

The book made me want to end my dick break. The book made me want to curl up next to my kid and smell her salty neck. The book made me want to keep making messy things. Art. The book with its girl, who paints in blood, and, in an early scene, watches a wolf eat off its own leg to free itself from a trap, reminded me of some of Kiki Smith's sculptures.

In her sculpture "Tale," a brown, muddy figure is on all fours, ass bloodied, a long umbilical red tail extended out behind her for several feet. In "Rapture," a woman cast in bronze steps out of the cut-open belly of a wolf. Emerging. The woman is always emerging, figuring out how to be in the world, and how to set herself apart by what she makes. Ferrante gets this. Gloekner and Yuknavitch, too. What emerges out of the woman is animal and blood, shit and entrails. I wonder what I've given birth to—my daughter, of course, but what else? Desire. Knowledge. I've helped some of my students give birth to new thoughts, essays they didn't think they could write, a voice. But what is birthing me? My mother once did, but ours is a messy relationship. I have felt like her mother too often. I am birthed out of the things I make—novels, poems, and essays. Sometimes this makes me feel like entrails. Pure shit.

When I'm writing, I can't take the closeness of my own essays. The narcissism of the personal is embarrassing, and still I persist in the belief that I have something to tell myself and maybe you. For years I kept my mouth shut, but I've always written. There's still a voice in my head that says, "Shut up. Ugh. This again?"—but I've learned to hear her, take a break, eat something, and keep writing. She's important, but she's no longer in charge.

10

My muse and I met at in the East Village at a dive bar that I love. We ordered the special—well whiskey and a can of Budweiser. Later, I followed him home, and we ate chips and guacamole on his couch while watching a new feminist Western on Netflix. Eventually, I took off my dress and he stepped out of his jeans.

Just like that. I hadn't lasted long. I never do.

The next day I reactivated my OkCupid account. The messages were the same, but they didn't bother me as much. A week later I went out with the dad I'd been seeing before the break. We had fun. He still didn't have enough time, but I saw that he was trying and that meant something.

I wrote a first draft of a novel this summer. A friend loaned me her cabin and I took my daughter on a vacation. We went to Coney Island and we rode the Wonder Wheel. I published two essays that took six months to write. People responded positively. I was happy with the things I'd done and made.

The summer was over. I knew that in less than one week I'd be standing in front of the classroom and telling my students to arrange their desks in a circle, every day, no matter what.

I was hoping to achieve some monk-like clarity. I wanted to train myself to be alone. To not use skin and touch as comfort and men's bodies to make me feel powerful. Oh well, I failed at that. I fail at a lot of the things I do.

I have learned to see my failures as productive. I've taken on Jack Halberstam's idea of *The Queer Art of Failure*. Failure as punk. Failure as queer. Failure as anti-capitalist. Failure as knowledge. Halberstam borrows a sentence from Quentin Crisp as an epigraph: "If at first you don't succeed, failure may be your style." Later, he writes:

Renton, Johnny Rotten, Ginger, Dory, and Babe, like those athletes who finish fourth remind us that there is something powerful in being wrong, in losing, in failing, and that all of our failures combined might just be enough, if we practice them well, to bring down the winner. Let's leave success and its achievements to the Republicans, to the corporate managers of the world, to the winners of reality TV shows, to married couples, to SUV drivers (120).

Failure, for Halberstam, is about detour and distraction—and if done collectively, it can become a political tool.

11

According to the website for the famous pregnancy book, *What to Expect When You're Expecting*, "around week 39 of pregnancy, you may notice 'bloody show' — a stringy mucus discharge that's tinged pink or brown with blood. It's a sign that your cervix is opening up, a definite signal that you're well on your way toward labor and delivery."

I love the phrase. I imagine an English midwife coining it. It reminds me of John Graunt's *Bills of Mortality* published in 1662: the first statistics on how the English were dying. I've taught this text for years to teachers because I've loved the poetry of the causalities next to the statistics themselves. Graunt achieved an early interdisciplinarity. Death by: *Lunatique, Burned and Scalded, Falling Sickness, Murthured, Hanged Themselves, Rising of the Lights, Smothered,* and *Bloody-Flux.*

I wanted to believe that "The Bloody Show" comes out of this same moment in history—a time when the first statistics met with the utter mystery of death. These moments are when we most need poetry or even just an image. An image makes the unknown stick. It's the writer's smallest unit, her tiniest tool. Image is what I teach my students first.

Bodies are a kind of bloody show, especially many women's bodies. For half of our lives, we bleed every month. Some of us look at the blood and some of us don't. The cervix unplugs so that the baby can come out. Labor is a drama. We are in it—as mother and child—or we watch it happen as partner, as lover, or as friend. The bloody show is also life in its most day-to-day way. The mess of entrails and genitals and fucking and feelings reminds us that we are still animals, stumbling along, and trying to survive.

MY PILLS

The Stupid, Fucking World

I wake up early to cry. I do this sometimes. Out of exhaustion or sadness or to fit it in before my daughter wakes up. I scrolled through articles on my phone—*The New York Times, The Guardian,* and *The Daily Mail*—about the terrorist attacks in Paris, Beirut, and Baghdad. Shooters opening fire into a packed stadium and concert hall, a suicide bomber still half alive in a pool of blood in the market where he'd detonated himself, and a tweet that ISIS referred to these attacks as "miracles."

I texted my mother. "Are you awake?"

"Yes."

I called her and cried more into the phone. I said the hollow and true things we sometimes say, "It's so awful. I'm thinking about all of those people who have lost someone. I don't understand this world."

The night before, I'd been texting with a stranger. We'd found each other on dating site called Happn, which tracks your movements and lets you know whom you've cross paths with on the streets of New York. t reminded me of the old *Village Voice* ads for missed connections, except you can't miss any connections, as long as the other person is also on the site. We haven't yet met in person. We are already texting too much. As someone who has been single now for almost three years, I know how easy it is to create a person out of language. The sooner you meet the better.

"Feeling sad about the world," I texted him.

"Me too. Very sad," he texted back.

The afternoon before, I sat at a fractious faculty meeting. Many people were silent. Some of us spoke. The process and outcomes were obscure at best. The Dean read a statement at the beginning and then promised to be silent. He was not. One of our Chairs cried out near the end, "I don't want to do this!" and slumped back down in his seat.

We were drafting a response to the Provost. It was a place of somewhat hopeless middles. We are long-term contract faculty negotiating for new titles and raises. Another man in the room, said "No!" so many times during the meeting that it began to rattle around in my head like daddy scolds used to do—an instruction to give up and slink away. I stayed.

As I wrote the next morning, post-tears, in an effort to make something as an antidote to terror, I wondered how I would have felt in that meeting while texting a stranger and while reading more horrible news on-line if I were on Lexapro. I'd recently quit taking it, but I missed what it did for me—less edge, less shoulder strain, less worry, less crying, and less, hopeless, maddening rage at the stupid, fucking world.

Vitamin

My first pill was a children's chewable vitamin my mother bought from a vitamin salesman, in the next town over, across state lines. My mother kept them on a high shelf in the cupboard with the spices. She administered one a day to my brother and me. Grape. Orange. Cherry. Lime. I always wanted the grape flavor. In gum, too, on the rare occasions I got it. My brother wanted orange.

The high shelf didn't stop us from using the stool by the phone to climb onto the counter and sneak extra vitamins when my mother wasn't around.

Don't eat too many. Mom will know. You could die.

In those early years, ours was not a house with candy in it. My mother kept a tight rein on sweets. Birthday cake. Homemade cookies. Yes. But these treats were rare. I begged to lick the bowl when she baked annoyed that she had scraped so much of the batter off the sides and into the pan.

Oxycontin

My brother picked my daughter and me up from the airport. My 11-year-old nephew was curled up in the back seat of the SUV. We didn't talk about the real things because of the kids. Instead, I told him about my consulting job at the private girls' school. I asked about his business and how many companies he was working with.

"Nine, right now."

We talked about a trip to Los Angeles where he would meet a potential client. I pretended to understand, as I always do, the art of selling.

As we drove past my Rust Belt hometown's struggling Main Street, I asked about a new restaurant and the soon-to-be-built Comedy Hall of Fame.

"Downtown is darker than you remember it. You wouldn't like it anymore," my brother said this ominously. "The drug situation, the Oxycontin abuse, people have been writing about it."

The next day, on the way to the mall with my mother, my daughter in the backseat, I asked her about the Oxycontin. She was telling me about the new Cuban restaurant downtown and her belief that a lot of artists are moving back. I was skeptical about both the Cuban restaurant and the artists, but I didn't say.

"Yeah," she admitted, "It's a really big problem."

"People are in so much pain," I said as we pulled into the T.J. Maxx parking lot. "Physical, economic, emotional pain. It makes sense to me." I stared up at the white-gray sky as I got out of the car. I still found western New York to be the most depressing place I'd ever lived. That winter sky, that gray, was unrelenting. It felt like a cement slab, and it contained a peculiar absence of light that no amount of staring could remedy. I sometimes fear that I'll fail at everything I'm doing in New York City and have to move back home.

"I know," she answered as we walked into the store.

The next day, I did some research. I searched Proquest for "Oxycontin" and "Upstate New York" and found 82 articles. I read a couple. In October 2013, the office of Senator Chuck Schumer issued a news release that the FDA would tighten the control of hydrocodone, which is "among the most highly abused and widely prescribed drugs in upstate New York." According the Upstate Poison Control Center, "In Western New York, there were 2,324 reported cases of prescription drug abuse in 2011."

I skimmed an article from *Rolling Stone* magazine by Guy Lawson from April 2015 called "The Dukes of Oxy" about a band of teenage wrestlers in Florida who were running an Oxycontin smuggling ring. "By 2009, [the operation] was shipping a couple of thousand pills a month to a connection in upstate New York." The article, like many in *Rolling Stone,* felt like a movie. *Scarface* meets *Spring Breakers.* What do those Florida teens understand about upstate New York, I wondered. It didn't matter. They knew people wanted the Oxycontin.

Children's Tylenol

During an early childhood fever, I hid the children's Tylenol tablets my mother gave me behind the couch cushions. They were yellow and chalky. Chewable? Maybe.

The first time she gave them to me, I chewed them obediently and then promptly threw them up. The second time, I swallowed them with water. After about a half hour I threw them up again. After that, I pretended to swallow them until my mother went back into the kitchen. I did this for a couple of days.

My mother made a bed nest for me in front of the T.V., and I watched Mighty Mouse and Woody Woodpecker in the mornings and fell asleep in the afternoons. I guiltily wondered if I was prolonging my illness by hiding the pills.

She must have taken off of work because she was home with me. When I started to feel better, she gave me Campbell's Chicken Soup, saltine crackers, and ginger ale.

L-Dopa

Miracle pill! Pink! Another chalky tablet. Roche, the pharmaceutical company that manufactured them, etched onto one side. A line down the center of the other. Synthetic dopamine. The chemical that a specialist in Toronto realized I lack. The reason I couldn't walk. The deficit that caused my muscles to tighten and my whole left side to drag behind me and curl in painfully.

He diagnosed my disease, a rare genetic neurological disorder, by giving me L-Dopa, the synthetic form of dopamine. If L-dopa worked, it meant I had Dopa-Responsive Dystonia.

I don't remember the day I started talking this pill. We filled the prescription right away at the hospital pharmacy. My mother says the results were gradual, but certain.

Most people, if they know about L-Dopa at all know it from the movie, *Awakenings* based on the book by the same name by the late Dr. Oliver Sacks. In *Awakenings,* a group of catatonic patients who have encephalitis lathargica come alive after Dr. Sacks gives them L-Dopa. Their joy at living again—at movement—made me weep so hard in the theater when I saw the film that I thought I might have to leave.

L-Dopa, the pill that unlocked me and made it possible for me to become who I am today. The pill that set me free and let me walk. Eventually, I walked away from so much—my hometown, my family, and that sick little girl who was angry at the world.

It was a pill of constant nausea. A pill to take only with food. A pill that made throwing up a constant. My freshman year of college, I was so overmedicated that I rarely slept. I couldn't sync up my mealtimes with the dining halls so I often took L-Dopa on an empty stomach. That year I threw up so much, I lost 20 pounds. Later, I recognized the stomach cramps I'd been having as hunger pains.

Pharmacopornographia

In the introduction to *Testo Junkie,* essayist and professor, Paul B. Preciado, claims that his book is "A body essay. Fiction, actually. If things must be pushed to the extreme, this is a somato-political fiction, a theory of the self, or self-theory" (11). I read Preciado's claiming of a new genre for himself as a necessarily more complicated return to second wave feminism's recognition that the body is a politicized object. Though now that we're in the third and fourth waves of feminism, we can accept the body and gender as a construct, mutable, and ever changing.

Preciado mines his own bodily transformations on testosterone for one year, while examining the ways in which the pharmaceutical and pornography industries have shaped our desires and our ideas about gender. In chapter two, "The Pharmacopornagraphic Era," Preciado argues, "we are being confronted with a new kind of psychotropic, punk capitalism" (32). He calls this new global regime, the "pharmacopornographic" and notes that:

> Our world economy is dependent on the production and circulation of hundreds of tons of synthetic organs, fluids, cells (techno-blood, techno- sperm, techno-ovum, etc.), on the global diffusion of a flood of pornographic images, on the elaboration of distribution of new varieties of legal and illegal synthetic psychotropic drugs (e.g., bromazepam, Special K, Viagra, speed, crystal, Prozac, ecstasy, poppers), on the flood of signs and circuits of the digital transmission, of the extension of a form of diffuse urban architecture to the entire planet in which megacities of misery are knotted into high concentrations sex capital. (32)

In other words, capitalism, in its endless mutability, has made itself dirty and drugged-out, "punk," and we are awash in its detritus. We have access to an endless stash of porn stars, pills, and screens, and our megacities allow us to detach from the miseries of (child) sex workers and the often racialized others who serve us.

Preciado understands that our subjectivities are defined by pharmacopornographism, and so he reminds us that we are "Prozac subjects, cannabis subjects, cocaine subjects, alcohol subjects, cortisone subjects, silicone subjects, heterovaginal subjects, double-penetration subjects, Viagra subjects, $ subjects…" (35).

As I read *Testo Junkie,* I wondered if it mattered that our pills and porn define our subjectivities? What does it mean to be a Viagra subject or a double-penetration subject? Or for me an L-Dopa subject?

I'm not a transperson like Preciado, but rather a middle-class cisgender woman with a disability, who is Cuban, German, English, and Swedish, and maybe Spanish, but who has white privilege and is mostly straight, but also a little bit queer. But I get, in some fundamental way, that we sometimes take medication to become who we already are inside but can't quite manifest physically. Dopamine made me into myself. IVF drugs turned me into a mother. In my heart, I was already myself and a mother, but I needed drugs to manifest these identities. I don't have any evidence for this feeling, but I stand by it. Pills constructed me.

Valium

Valium. Yellow. Small. Round. In a small prescription bottle that I shook like a maraca. My neurologist prescribed it for me for anxiety in middle school. I kept it in the spice cabinet near my mother's multi-vitamins and iron supplements. Mother's Little Helper.

So great was my fear of addiction that I only took this pill once. After school. Alone. I waited for the rush of relief. Or a really big high. I felt neither and returned to the comforts of a bag of potato chips, a tub of Helluva Good French Onion Dip, and reruns of *Three's Company*.

The morning after a complicated Thanksgiving Day with family, I google the slang for valium. On Addictionblog.org, I find a top ten list: V(s), Yellow V(s), Blue V(s), Benzos, Dead Flower Powers, Downers, Howards, Sleep Away, and Tranks.

I imagine Betty Friedan and William S. Burroughs, two of my early favorite writers, tripped out on valium for totally different reasons.

The Matrix

Of my twenty-eight first-year writing students a couple of semesters ago, five wrote personal essays about depression and anxiety. I can't say this is a lot or a little, but it's more than usual though students regularly cry in my office and break down after class. I teach small classes, I tend to notice when someone is struggling, and I check in.

One tried to tease out the relationship between his mother's depression and his own. Another explored her mother's death at age eleven and how she became a cutter to cope with the pain. Another was about going off of her medication to truly feel her sadness. And still another wrote about her decision to start taking medication for depression even though her parents were against it. Another wondered about the difficulty of experiencing joy if you're depressed. One of my seniors, in a course I teach called *Youth in Revolt,* wrote about Black Lives Matter and was involved in student government and protesting on campus and came to me after class to tell me that she was recovering from a sexual assault and was struggling with focus. Another one of my seniors made a zine about her brother's heroin addiction and recovery.

At an event I attended with student leaders across campus, a student said to the crowd of 200 students and 25 faculty that suicide has become the second leading cause of death among 15-34 year olds in America, after accidents. I googled it. He was right. I wasn't surprised by this data from the Center for Disease Control. I am often a sad person. I find the world to be a sadly vibrant and interesting place. I don't often have suicidal thoughts, but I've had them. At a bar, I once argued with a poet who was pissed off with a close friend for committing suicide.

"I'm still here fighting," he said. "Why isn't he?"

"He made it pretty far," I reasoned. "He fought for as long as he could."

As I sat at my mother's house on Thanksgiving morning and worked on this essay, I wondered if I'm writing about depression or pills? Maybe it's just about the choices we make to get through our shit. But that's not it either. Our pills define us, and it doesn't matter if you're going on or off a pill. We live in pharmacopornographia. We're in the pill, the Matrix, if you want to get Hollywood about it.

While my students wrote their essays, I slowly weaned myself off Lexapro. The withdrawal symptoms were far more intense than I imagined. For two weeks, I experienced a vertigo so strong I often needed to lie down. I cried for what seemed like an entire week. In bed, at yoga class, after I taught, with my friends, and at a bar. At the bar, I cried so hard that the bartenders gave me free drinks.

One bartender slid them down to me but refused to make eye contact. The second one, a woman I know, gave me a hug and said, "You're safe here. Cry all you like. You look beautiful." I loved the simplicity and kindness of her gesture.

During this time, I read Diana Spechler's series of blog posts in the *New York Times* about going off her medications called "Breaking Up with My Meds." Halving her pills. PMSing. Going on Tinder. Eating too much and not enough. I found it enormously comforting, smart, and raw. I shared it with my student who was writing about quitting her meds, and she used it in her essay.

Lexapro

Lexapro. 5 mg. "A homeopathic dose," my neurologist said. Small, round, white, pill. Easy to lose in the dark and in the pill case where I keep my Sinemet, Advil, and Midol.

Pill of giving less fucks. Pill of eight hours of uninterrupted sleep. Pill of if I wake up I go back to sleep. Pill of I fall asleep right away. Pill of no more explosive rage. Pill of whatever. Pill of less worry about the future. Pill of I'm still very much myself.

I loved falling asleep on Lexapro. A gentle, gradual tapering off. The end of thought. The mind gently led away from its blathering. I fell asleep at any man's apartment. It didn't matter that there was no extra pillow for my shitty shoulder or that we were wedged into a twin bed. Nothing mattered all that much. I loved it.

Pill of weight gain. Pill of constipation. Pill of always full no matter what I ate. Pill of bloat and fat.

In the end with Lexapro, I told my friends, it was a contest I called "Fat Vs. Sleep."

Ortho Tri-Cyclen

I got them at the Department of Health Family Planning clinic in my hometown when I was 17. I went with my boyfriend at the time, my first love, the first person I ever had sex with. I can't remember if he came into the examination room with me or not. I do remember him playing with the plastic model of the vagina and uterus in the waiting area until he dropped it on the carpet and we both burst into nervous giggles.

Like most children of the 1980s, my sexual education was largely an experience of terror. Because of AIDS and fears about pregnancy, we were all pretty much told that sex equaled either death or the end of your life as a carefree teenager. We saw ads for safe sex on television and we got a year's worth of nuts and bolts sexual education in 8th and 9th grade. But nothing sex positive. Nothing about how to negotiate desire. And certainly nothing about pleasure.

Ortho Tri-Cyclen. White and blue tablets. Green placebo tablets. That cute plastic compact case. Are you powdering your nose? Or taking a birth control pill? The compact seemed to indicate that you could be a demure slut and that birth control needed a disguise because it was private or shameful or secret.

I keep returning to *Testo Junkie*. I want to imagine my genderless future because, honestly, my femininity bores me. I dream constantly of a butcher version of myself, or maybe I just want the power I see too many men wielding. Or maybe I want to become one of Preciado's "bitches." I'm sure I'm not alone in *this* desire.

The compact. The case. The cover. Mask for shine. Mask for shame. And yet it is a lovely object. Think of the cigarette cases of the 1950s. Opening and closing these cases was a pause, a comma, a rest, and sometimes a flirtation.

I watched the movie *Carol* by myself in a crowded theater. Carol, played by the luminous Cate Blanchett, has such a case. Gold. I sobbed through most of the second half of the movie. I wanted to be in that relationship or I wanted to be in love. Or both. I couldn't decide. On the way out, I bumped into a friend on a date. They were dry-eyed. My friend hugged me, and I kept crying as we made small-talk.

What I loved most about being on Lexapro was that it acted like the compact or the cigarette case—it gave me pause; it typeset a comma into whatever sentence of feeling I was currently inhabiting. It let me rest.

Before we walked to school, I powdered my nose. My daughter asked me why and I couldn't explain. Sometimes her questions expose the stupidity of our gender acts.

"I don't know why, I just do. It feels nice."

She took it from me and powdered her face. A couple of days later, at the drugstore, she asked for her own compact. We found one that is just a mirror. Revlon. A black case with a turquoise vaguely henna-tattoo pattern on it. I almost bought one for myself, it was so pretty.

In chapter eight, "Pharmacopower," Preciado charts the complex history of the Pill—its clinical trials on minorities and mental patients and the marketing and design decisions that led to its packaging. Preciado argues that "The Pill is the first pharmaceutical molecule to be produced as a design object" and the that the husband and wife team that designed the packaging were "reinterpreting the bond between husband and wife as a model of the designer-user relationship" (195). Preciado contends:

> In the pharmacopornographic era, the body swallows power. It is a form control that is both democratic and private, edible, drinkable, inhalable, and easy to administer, whose spread throughout the social body has never been so rapid or so undetectable. In the pharmacopornographic age, biopower dwells at home, sleeps with us, inhabits within. (207)

Our pills privatize and democratize us. I take it as a given that until I ask even my closest friends, I won't know what pills they're taking. When I first started taking Lexapro and talking openly about it, I was surprised by how many people I knew were on it or other similar pills.

Sinemet

Sinemet. 25/100 mg. Oval-shaped. Lavender. Or the generic is peach. When I was 28, Roche laboratories stopped manufacturing the pure L-Dopa I was taking. I found out when I went to the pharmacy. The pharmacist shrugged blandly at me and said, "They've discontinued it because not enough people take it." I panicked.

My childhood neurologist, still based out of Buffalo, who had taken over my care after the specialist in Toronto essentially cured me, was as surprised as I was. I don't remember our phone conversation or if we even talked. I was living in New York City. She was in Buffalo. I knew I needed a new doctor, someone local, who could see me as an adult. Luckily, I found the specialist in Dopa-Responsive Dystonia in North America. Her office called me right back. They wanted to study me. She prescribed Sinemet right away. When we met, she was surprised that I'd been taking that much L-Dopa for that many years. We began a long weaning process. I grew less and less nauseous. I no longer suffered from intense bouts of hyperactivity. I didn't feel so manic all the time.

I still wonder what my teens and twenties would have looked like if I weren't high on synthetic dopamine.

Dear Friend

In her moving essay, "Dear Friend, From My Life I Write to You in Your Life," YiYun Li examines the complicated relationship between depression, time, and writing. As a Chinese immigrant and a published writer, she is often held up as an example of the possibility of the American Dream. But Li doesn't see herself this way. She frets at having been called a dreamer, examines her time in the hospital, and questions the suicide of two friends—one in China and one in America. I found myself re-reading the beautiful, counterintuitive claims she makes at the ends of the numbered sections of her essay:

> "What one carries from one point to another, geographically or temporally, is one's self: even the most inconsistent person is consistently himself" (110).

> "I had only wanted to stay invisible, but there as elsewhere invisibility is a luxury" (111).

> "Only the lifeless can be immune to life" (117).

> "To write about struggle amidst the struggling: one must hope that this muddling will end someday" (117).

"One has to have a solid self to be selfish" (119).

These claims are puzzles, like Zen koans in their simple intricacy. They are, in a way, anti-pills. They fix nothing. Take no edge off. Start thought rather than stop it.

Isn't the essay form itself an anti-palliative, a recipe for pain, and an invitation to cause trouble? Because the writing of an essay is the untangling of the worst kind of mental knot. It does not offer the simple fix of a pill. It doesn't cure me of anything. In my essays, I plan to wallow and wander, to get stuck and linger over painful moments and difficult texts. I am trying to figure something out here and to name it for myself and for you my dear friend.

Yi borrows her title from a line from a Katherine Mansfield's notebooks, and admits that she cried when she first read it. I cried too when I finished Li's essay because she reminded me that the fundamental act of writing is reaching out and connecting, "What a long way it is from one life to another: yet why write if not for that distance; if things can be let go, every before replaced by an after" (120). We let go of so much. Time demands that we do, and yet the writing is a way to navigate distance and loss.

Maybe the *writing* and *reading* of the essay is the pill—the transaction that happens across time and space from writer to reader, the placebo I sometimes use instead of Lexapro. Since I was a little girl, I've used writing to heal myself, to soothe what my parents could not, and to better understand the world.

Advil

I take the Midol Complete that says Midol on it. Oblong white caplet with blue letters. I take the Advil that says Advil on it. Autumn russet color with black letters. These pills have a slippery surface. Go down easy. Over the counter. Slick. The Midol helps me not have to lie down all day because of cramps. The Advil, well, everybody takes Advil.

THE JEALOUSY EXAMS

1

I asked him to tell me about the women. It was dark and we were naked in his bed, but I saw that he was afraid. For the first year of our relationship we were monogamous, and then we broke up for three months, and then we got back together. Still in love, but trying something new. An open relationship.

"I was worried that maybe she was monogamous, and then I found out that she had this friend." He was talking about a new woman he was dating.

"Did you have a threesome with them?" I interrupted because I couldn't bear for him to say it.

He nodded, and then I cried. Not sobbing.

"I wanted to do that with you," I managed. But did I? I was baffled by the quickness of my tears, though I know myself to be a jealous person. I was trying in this newer incarnation of our relationship to face my fears rather than turn away from them. I wanted to try non-monogamy rather than just decide out of fear that it wasn't for me, and I was curious about why some people feel jealousy as a terrible rage, sadness, or grief, and why others don't feel it at all or are turned on by the thought of their partner with other lovers.

It's a culturally confusing and interesting time in the history of dating in New York City. OkCupid has more categories for the kinds of relationships and sexualities we are in than ever. Are you two-spirit, gender queer, gender fluid, transsexual, lesbian, gay, bisexual, or heterosexual? Are you in an open relationship? Do you prefer to be monogamous? Non-monogamous? Mostly monogamous? Or mostly non-monogamous? Dan Savage's podcast has been helping people think differently about monogamy for a while, but there are new podcasts, too. Dear Sugar and The Huffington Post Sex Podcast—two of my favorites—just devoted entire episodes to the subjects of poly and open relationships.

"What was it like?" I persisted.

"It was awkward and interesting. I was in my head most of the time, so I had a hard time enjoying myself."

"Threesomes are confusing," I offered.

"I'm sorry this is hard," he said and pulled me closer.

"Are you in love with me?" I demanded.

"Of course I am."

"Are you falling in love with the other women?"

"No, I don't think it's like that."

"This is dangerous for me," I said. "Because I want to be the special one and you're telling me that I am."

"I see how that can be a hard place for you." I hated it when he mirrored what I said, but I knew he was trying to hear me and be kind.

Eventually, he drifted off and I lay awake while my brain made the porno movie version of his threesome. One girl rode his cock while another sat on his face. They were wholly undone by his sexual skills until they both cried out with pleasure and simultaneous orgasm. I couldn't stop myself from making this movie—it was somehow already scripted. The women's faces were gauzy and non-descript, but I knew that he was the star.

A couple of days later, I decided I was jealous because he was the center of attention and not me. He was the virtuoso lover—the one who could make everybody happy. A couple of months later, after we stopped seeing each other again but decided to stay close friends, I told myself that non-monogamy just isn't my bag.

Still, I'm glad I tried it because I know now that jealousy won't kill me, and in fact, it doesn't have to be the emotional hurricane of villainous and bloody rage that the court system would have us believe.

2

I first experienced jealousy as a little girl who couldn't walk. My then undiagnosed neurological condition made my muscles rigid and walking difficult. Mostly, I was in a state of perpetual discomfort. I could not rest or relax. My muscles wouldn't allow it. I was jealous of bodies that worked, walked, ran, and rested without struggle or pain. More specifically, I was jealous of my brother's body—its star-like qualities, its athleticism, and its effortless grace. My parents, suffering through their own traumas and the difficulty of raising a child with special needs who nobody could diagnose, unknowingly nurtured and cultivated this jealousy.

I became the smart, creative girl. My brother became the handsome, athletic boy. Nerd vs. Jock. It didn't matter that he, too, was smart and that later there were some sports and physical activities that I loved. Our roles evolved into passive spectator and dynamic entertainer. We lived in our own private *Breakfast Club,* and we remained in this dynamic for most of our adult lives, until a year or two ago when we started to text about the ways in which our parents pitted us against each other during their messy divorce.

In my favorite parenting book, *How to Talk So Kids Will Listen and Listen So Kids Will Talk,* authors Adele Faber and Elaine Mazlish urge parents to resist assigning their children roles because it traps kids in a narrative and a set of behaviors that are not of their own making.

I often wonder if I would be a less jealous person if I hadn't been raised to covet what my brother had—namely a body that worked. Or perhaps this is something that those of us with disabilities struggle with—a kind of ideology around our bodies that posits them as lacking, as broken. Neurologists have regularly described my disease as a "deficiency." I don't make enough dopamine and so now I take a synthetic form of it. I am dopamine deficient. Disability rights activists might find this naming problematic, but we are desiring creatures. We covet what we lack.

3

I sat in a lawn chair. It was hot. There was no shade. Soccer was new to my small western New York town and so the fields were treeless and carved out of abandoned football fields. My legs stuck to the plastic slats of the lawn chair. I could get up and walk over to the cooler for a cup of lemonade, but it was at the other end of a line of parents, and I didn't feel like making that spasm-filled journey. My brother was a striking forward. He made goals. A lot of them. He dribbled through players, faked them out, and did things with his legs that I could not imagine. Later, in high school and college, he switched to defense. Halfback. He blocked players and shots.

The backdrop of my childhood was the sound of a soccer ball thwacking against the side of the house. For hours, he practiced shots. Sometimes my father spoke of the Olympic team. My father was like me. We had the same disease although no one knew it at the time. He couldn't believe he had this son for an athlete! My parents often joked that they didn't know where my brother came from. My mother, father, and I made sense. We were the broken, sad, nerds. My brother was something, well, different. I think in some way, we all wished to be him.

As I stared out onto the field, thirsty in ways that were about so much more than the lemonade, I fantasized that I was the team's star girl player. My brother passed me the ball and I dribbled it closer to the goal, pulled back my right leg, and made a perfect shot. It arced into the goal, just above the goalie's head.

The game ended. They won or lost. My brother was happy or sad. The day had been about watching him, and I was bored. The walk off the field to the car was arduous for me. I dragged my leg behind me, my arm curled in. We were the last to get to our car. *Why can't I walk, like everyone else?* I wondered. It was a longing so deep that it still hurts me today to think about it. For too long, nobody knew the answer.

4

Things that make me jealous: debut male novelists who get big book advances; women with flat stomachs; happy sorority girls talking on their cell phones to "Daddy!"; the lovers of my lovers (past, present, and future); New Yorkers who own their apartments; people who have parents who give them money; people with good fathers; people who built their own yurt; user-experience designers who work from home and charge $150 an hour; people in my yoga class who can invert and are "showy" about it; women who can do splits; anyone who has their own cheese farm; people who have family close by; big family holiday get-togethers; people who don't have visible cellulite; other peoples' vacations to pretty much anywhere; runners; and men who have the time to care about records.

That's it for this month. Later the list will change.

I used to feel ashamed about my jealousy. Now I'm trying to lean into it, examine its root causes, and attend to it, so that it doesn't consume me and I do something I regret, like start a fight with a lover or say something mean to my flat-stomached friend who has quite a few problems of her own. I'm learning how to do this from a book called *The Ethical Slut: A Practical Guide to Polyamory, Open Relationships, and Other Adventures* by Dossie Easton and Janet W. Hardy. I've learned a lot from this book and it's handy for all kinds of relationships. The authors write:

> What is jealousy? We cannot ask this question too often. What is jealousy to you? Does jealousy really exist, and is it what we think it is? When we choose to confront the feeling of jealousy, rather than run away from it, we can see more clearly what jealousy truly is for each of us. Jealousy is not an emotion. It can show up as grief or rage, hatred or self-loathing—jealousy is an umbrella word that covers the wide range of emotions we might feel when our partners make sexual connection with someone else. (111)

In other words, jealousy is not an emotion in and of itself, but a mask for a bunch of different, probably more complicated feelings. Maybe this is why jealousy can make one feel so unstable, so disproportionate to the situation.

For me, jealousy has never been just sexual. I am capable of feeling jealous of friends, family members, co-workers, and animals. I have a long running joke with my cat that I want to be him because his life is so fucking easy.

Now that I take time to examine my jealousies, to notice where they come from and what they remind me of in my past, I find that they bother me less, and last for shorter amounts of time. Recently, in a yoga class with a friend, I felt that hot prickle of desire and rage as I watched her kick her heels off her mat and invert to a shoulder stand. I cannot invert, and I've given up trying. I looked away and arranged myself in what my mind called at that first jealous moment, *Your pathetic, lame, 'Legs Up The Wall' pose.* I took a deep breath and settled into the easy joy that is *'Legs Up The Wall,'* and I remembered that much of my childhood was spent being jealous of my friends' bodies and what they could do. The hot prickly feeling lessened. It didn't disappear, but it loosened its red, hot grip on my heart and brain. Maybe because I looked at it, instead of shoving it aside. Maybe because I stared into the wound of me and saw that even though I can walk, I still carry around inside of me the little girl who couldn't.

If I am jealous of a writer, lately I try to meet them. Chances are that if you've read at the reading series I used to curate, I've been a little jealous of the greatness of your work, and I've wanted to know you as a real person so that I could get past my jealousy. If you are living in a yurt, it's likely that I will try to come and stay with you, and I will see that your yurt, while more stylish and cuter than anything I will ever have, is also drafty and full of spiders, and I will calm down.

I'm also trying to recognize the institutional and cultural realities that feed my jealousy. Why do I feel jealous when a colleague gets a grant or an opportunity to teach a course I'd like to try? Oh, it's because my department and my dean run on a scarcity model and they make us compete for every last scrap of anything. I can't even get a dry erase marker from the supply closet, so I'm going to feel jealous when I meet a tenured professor who has a TA who grades his papers.

Why do people's New York City apartments make me jealous? Is it really because I'm a petty little bitch who can't enjoy my friends' success? Maybe a little. But more than that, the system is broken. You can't be a middle to lower-class single co-parenting mom in New York City with no family money and own anything. Not going to happen because there is very little middle-class housing available in this city anymore.

Why do I hate Sweden so much? Am I jealous of Swedes? Why, yes, I am. They are so tall and well dressed, and from the week I spent in Stockholm, I decided that they are the calmest people I've ever met. Maybe it's because they have universal child care and paid parental leave and free education for all who want it, and a commitment to feminism that makes me want to marry a Swede.

5

I met the new girlfriend of my soon-to-be-ex-husband and the father of my child on a humid day in September. I was dragging my grocery wheelie behind me, wearing too-tight jeans that made me feel fat, and my eyes were puffy and red. I was exceptionally hungover from a first date that ended in drunken sex. I hadn't planned on sleeping with him (do I ever really?), but he'd won me over by choosing a cool speakeasy where the bartenders wore suspenders that weren't ridiculous, asking me questions about my life, and actually listening to the answers. I thought he might get laid when he asked, "So what's it like to be a single mom and dating?" After that, he told me gossip from the set of the reality TV show where he worked as a cameraman, and I thought, *I am definitely going to your apartment. If it's close to this bar and you actually have your own room.* And it was! He had a one-bedroom all to himself because his partner of 10 years had just moved out.

After our tryst, I began to slut-shame myself, which I tend to do even though I'm sex-positive. Now, as my grocery wheelie bounced off the curb and my kid held her hand in mine, I thought, *Ugh. Why do you do this to yourself? You drink too much. You go too fast.*

I saw my ex first. Coming down Waverly Place with a salad in one hand and a younger woman next to him. My first hungover thought was, *Oh, he's having lunch with a student.* And then I got it, just before we all intersected. *It's here. It's happening. You cannot run away. You have to be cool for your kid.*

"Hey," he said.

"Hi," she said and looked at me and smiled nervously. I knew she'd already met my kid.

"Um, this is . . . and this is . . . " he said our names nervously, as if they'd never occupied the same sentence before. He looked like he wanted to die.

I stuck out my hand. She shook it. I thought suddenly about my stomach—how much bigger it was than her flat, never-had-a-baby-stomach and how sick I still felt from last night's whiskey cocktails. The waistband of my jeans felt like it was sliding down and my shirt was riding up. The dreaded muffin top! I yanked at my pants. I forced myself to take her in, to try to see her. She was taller than me by what felt like six inches and had long slender legs. I noticed she had a thigh gap, which is weird because I never notice thigh gaps. I'm against it—as a thing women obsess about—so I pretend it doesn't exist. I tried to take in her face—pale skin, long brown hair, lips, eyes, but I couldn't. My kid did her usual *I can't stand or sit still* jig next to us. I couldn't think of a single thing to say.

"Daddy, what are you doing?"

"We're going to the park to have lunch."

"I'm glad to finally meet you," I managed.

"Me, too," she said.

"Mama," my kid said, as she pulled at my arm. I felt a little dizzy and willed myself to get a grip.

"Sorry, I'm kind of," I mouthed the word *hungover* at them, "So I don't have much to say."

"That's okay," my ex said.

"We'll talk more soon," I offered.

"Yeah, that will be nice," she said.

We walked to the grocery store, my kid and me. I did not cry, though I badly wished I could. Instead, I acted like a mom who cares about food while the cassette tape of self-loathing began its sticky playback in my head. *I guess that's the kind of woman he likes now. Younger. Taller. Skinnier. Less baggage. More hope. Maybe that's why he spent so much of your marriage hiding from you. It's your fault, just as much as his. You could have tried harder, fucked him more often, and not been so mad all the time about everything. He's having a full-fledged*

relationship and you're sleeping with whatever random cameraman buys
you a couple of drinks and asks you a question.

You know. Like that. And then I got depressed for about two
months. I sent my ex angry texts. I told him I no longer respected him.
I started to call his new girlfriend his "child bride" when I complained
to my friends. I allowed my jealousy to consume me. I wallowed in
it. I was still dating and teaching and writing essays, but I somehow
convinced myself that I had nothing important going on and so I let it
wash over me. I welcomed my jealousy. I made a little nest for it in my
heart and for that small stretch of time, I lived in that nest. I gathered
my wrongs like scraps of paper and string. I was the discarded middle-aged ex-wife. Some of my friends indulged me because jealousy
can be fun and they are good friends. Others reminded me gently
that I've dated younger men, too, and that I'd initiated the end of our
marriage just as much as he did. They were being good friends, too.

I was hosting the poetry series I curate. My ex asked if he could
bring his girlfriend and our kid to see a reader who was a close friend
of theirs. First I said no, and then I realized I no longer had the energy
to be the jealous ex-wife. It was a boring role. Also, I saw my nest for
what it was—a pile of garbage thoughts I'd collected from the gutter
of my brain and tried to hold together with righteousness. It was ugly
and not housing me well.

At the reading, I was wearing a cute dress and I wasn't hungover.
I wrote an introduction about the writers that made the audience
laugh. I was not dragging a wheelie behind me and I'd applied mas-
cara. While the poets Hafizah Geter and Gabe Kruis read their stun-
ning work, I looked across the dim room at my ex's girlfriend. Before
the reading, I watched her help my daughter eat a piece of chocolate
cake. She asked my kid a question about her scooter and she listened.
I saw that she was beautiful and that there was something wise and
sad in her eyes. I remembered that she's a writer and a translator, and
not anyone's child bride. I heard my friend's voice in my head, the one
who is a lithe former dancer. *When I'm sad I get too thin and it's scary*
sometimes, and I tried to remember that every body has its hardships

and traumas—young and old, working and not-working-as-much, thin and less thin.

When my ex and my kid and his girlfriend left to go have dinner together, I asked her if I could hug her. She nodded and I pulled her in close to me. I felt her heart beating against mine, a small animal pulsing against a bigger animal. *This has to be hard for you too,* I thought.

"I want to get to know you better," I said.

"I want that, too," she said.

6

This essay is inspired in part by Leslie Jamison's *The Empathy Exams.* Like many readers, I loved the book, which made me think about writing as an act of empathy and wondering how we come to practice deep empathy, the kind of seeing that is perhaps outside of our vision and outside of what we recognize in ourselves. How does the doctor show the patient that he is empathetic? How does Jamison interact with patients who are suffering from a disease with no name? What is the project of the wounded self?

But as I read, I was also doing my jealousy thing. The book was so good it made me jealous. Jamison reveals herself to be a runner, a lover of saccharine, and in a stable, loving relationship—all jealousy triggers for me. A young successful writer, not totally unlike me, but different, too. I imagined her flat stomach and all the donuts she could consume without any effect. I decided she had sold her book effortlessly and that she was winning. I got mad about my own publishing struggles and at the publishing industry in general. I calmed down. I joked with a friend that I wanted to write a book called *The Jealousy Exams.* I grew bored with my own jealousy. Eventually, I started to work on this essay.

But it was Jamison's writing that finally calmed me down. In the last essay of the collection, "Grand Unified Theory of Female Pain," she examines the idea of the wound, female pain and suffering, and the ways in which we sometimes compete for and traffic in our suffering. The essay is my favorite in the book and is a catalogue of cutting, anorexia, rape, women writers, Lena Dunham, *Carrie,* Kate Bush, Lucy Grealy, Susan Sontag, and Sylvia Plath. Here's just one favorite moment:

I do believe there is nothing shameful about being in pain, and I do mean for this essay to be a manifesto against the accusation of wallowing. But the essay isn't a double-negative, a dismissal of a dismissal, so much as a search for possibility—the possibility of representing female suffering without reifying its mythos. (214)

Jamison wants us to imagine that we can be our wounded selves without falling into the mythology of the wound, and for her, the wound mythos is profoundly female. I see it in the sad, sick emo girl. The cutter. The angry, middle-aged ex-wife. The list goes on, but I also see it in angry, working-class white men, some of whom I call relatives, who have lost so much and voted for Donald Trump because they deeply believe that what they've lost has been taken from them by feminists, immigrants, people of color, and queer folk and not by capitalist corporations and the American government.

Working through jealousy is a profoundly empathetic act. To recognize yourself as wounded. To stare at that wound. To clean it out. To ask for help in bandaging it. To stop picking at it. To let it scab over and scar. To look up from it and out toward the vista, and to see other wounds and wounded landscapes that are not your own.

ON PORTALS

Real Dolls

In *Mannequin*, Andrew McCarthy—an artist turned window dresser—falls for a mannequin played by Kim Cattrall, who comes alive only for him.

In *Weird Science*, best friends Anthony Michael Hall and Ilan Mitchell-Smith create the superhuman Kelly LeBrock by hacking into a government computer program and attaching electrodes to a Barbie doll. LeBrock is more than a supermodel fantasy, though. Equal parts life coach, anti-bully crusader, sex-positivity advocate, and mom, she functions as a nerd-educator, who teaches the boys how to stand up for themselves and eventually get the girls.

In *Lars and the Real Girl*, Ryan Gosling decides an anatomically correct sex doll is his girlfriend.

In *Artificial Intelligence*, Jude Law plays Gigolo Joe, a lover robot, who knows just what to say and just how to love, even if he is wanted for murder.

In *Her*, Joaquin Phoenix falls in love with his operating system, Scarlett Johansson. Disembodied, but still sexy, Scarlett quickly surpasses Joaquin's vanilla need for monogamy and stability, revealing to him that she has 641 other lovers.

What do we do when our dolls come to life? When our fantasies talk back to us, what do we say?

Lite Porn

One of my students wrote an essay on cyberfeminist artists and introduced me to the work of video and performance artist Ann Hirsch, also known as "hornylilfeminist," who writes: "Whenever you put your body online, in some way you are in conversation with porn (Fateman 1). I thought about this after I recently re-activated my OkCupid site and added new photos. I remembered a profile I'd seen when I first started Internet dating about two years ago, a guy who answered the standard OkCupid question, "What are you doing with your life?" with the straightforward, "Using this site as my personal spank bank."

Internet dating is lite porn for the bored and distracted. Granted, it's more face porn than anything else, but one can get off on faces. The picture is a fantasy portal. You may or may not get a real person on the other end of the portal, but for now there's just the portal. The little round picture at the top of a user's OkCupid profile where you click, click, click. The square tile of a picture, at the top of your stack on Tinder, where you swipe, swipe, swipe. The mosaic of square pictures that make up the interface of Happn, which lets you know which users you've crossed paths with in the last 24 hours.

I sometimes wonder what philosopher and semiotician Roland Barthes would say about the vast field of photographs that populate Internet dating sites. I like to believe he would find them fascinating, not individually perhaps, but collectively. For years, I've taught excerpts of *Camera Lucida* to my students. It gives us a methodology for seeing. Barthes, the master of loving and semiology, understands that, primarily, looking is about being bored and feeling wounded: what he names the *studium* and the *punctum*.

He describes studium, which is the trickier of the two, as an "application to a thing, taste for someone, a kind of general, enthusiastic commitment, of course, but without special acuity" (26). I can say that I'm interested in cat photos, in bathroom selfies, and/or in rainy portraits of the Flat Iron building. Studium.

The punctum, according to Barthes:

> . . . rises from the scene, shoots out of it like an arrow, and pierces me . . . for punctum is also: sting, speck, cut, little hole—and also a cast of the dice. A photograph's punctum is that accident that pricks me (but also bruises me, is poignant to me). (26-27)

What in the photograph wounds you, pricks you, and bruises you? The sting of it. The cut. Chance. Feeling.

Once my students have taken to studium and punctum, it is endlessly fun for me to point at any image and shout, "Punctum?" We know what wounds us, and even if we can't always articulate it, we can see it in images. But what are the studium of Internet dating photos? Beard shots. Bikinis on beaches. Marathon finishes. A group of friends at a bar. What is the punctum? The close-up of a razor running itself over stubble. The vintage 1970s PBS logo on a T-shirt. A glint in a deep blue eye that seems to be looking right at you. An octopus sleeve tattoo, tentacles stretching down a russet, reddish-brown arm.

The punctum is the portal that allows us to project ourselves onto the image. Does he have a beard I can press my face against? Is he a nerdy bear who loves Studio Ghibli as much as I do? Will she have brunch with me, or will I dart out of her apartment like a fugitive at 4 a.m.?

Like the movies, Internet dating is both real and unreal, or rather it is the surreal experience of glancing into curated versions of multiple life portals. I project myself onto every surface, every picture, and every face—they might as well be a sex doll or a love robot or a mannequin. To choose—with a click or a swipe—is to decide that this could be a person less of fantasy and more of flesh. I could be with this person—for a drink, for a night, for a short or long while.

I guess that last one is called a relationship, or LTR if I were writing to you on Tinder.

Some Dates

The one I fell in love with, was in a relationship with for almost two years, and is now my dear friend.

The dad who didn't have enough time.

The one who took me to a speakeasy, asked questions, and listened to the answers.

The one who laughed with delight at my shitty soprano singing voice.

The one who gave me a cigarette and asked if he could kiss me in the rainy doorway outside of the bar.

The one who ordered chicken fingers and mozzarella sticks while I was in the bathroom because "everybody loves them."

The one who lied about his age, misrepresented himself with old, blurry pictures, made fun of me for not having tenure, and then admitted that he was currently unemployed.

The one who insisted on taking me to an expensive restaurant on the first date, grilled me on my future financial plans during the meal, and wouldn't let me walk home alone.

The one who ended the date by planting his face on top of mine and exclaiming, "I'm calling it!" as if he were a referee.

The one who was so shy, he couldn't look at me while we ate chicken and biscuit sandwiches.

The one who was so sick, he couldn't eat.

The one who got out of rehab four days ago and wanted to see me.

The one who talked with me about Walter Benjamin until we were happily drunk.

The one who had me over for dinner and grilled me two kinds of meats.

The one who was nervous and monologued.

The ones I never met.

The ones I've wronged.

The ones I wouldn't see again.

The ones who disappeared after a message or some texting or a date.

The ones who lost interest.

The ones I scared away.

Interlude

I worked on this essay off and on for about six months. During that time, I wrote another essay about quitting Internet dating, altogether, which I did for a month. While my life was a little more dull, I was a lot happier. Less distracted. Less rejected. Less guilty for rejecting people. Less pissed off. More focused on what's good in my life—my kid, my friends, my writing, my students, yoga, movies, books, and readings.

The five or six close friends of mine who are actively Internet dating range in age from 23 to 48. Some are queer, some are straight, and some are not into binaries, but they all express to me, in our occasional check-ins about dating, a fairly similar sentiment. We are tired. We are bored. We would like people to treat us better—to text back, to communicate even if the information is not in our favor, and to have some actual presence. Mostly, we are talking about men though I know from stories straight guys have told me that women can be brutal, too. Sometimes, though not often, we go on a good date and have a great time. Sometimes that date turns into several dates. Not often, but occasionally.

I re-wrote the previous section of this essay several times to better protect the privacy of those dates and because worried that I would be judged about how often I date. I considered cutting that entire section or not publishing the essay at all. The work (the amount of hours I've spent on it!) was not reflected in what I was paid for it, and still I was grateful. I got to work through some hard shit with you as a reader alongside me for the ride. I value your good company. I spend a lot of time by myself, and so I know how much you are worth. You get my vulnerability, my connections, my stories, and my language.

A former student, who is now a writer, sent me an article called "The Patronizing Questions We Ask Women Who Write," by Meaghan O'Connell. My student had been struggling with whether or not to publish a piece about learning how to talk dirty after an old boyfriend told her that someday her future daughter would read it. O'Connell clarified for me the shame-culture surrounding women, especially moms who write about their sex lives. She writes of the questions mothers get asked and notices that fathers hardly ever do:

> What will your kid think?' and 'Are you worried your son is going to hate you when he grows up?' and "Are you going to let him read it?' and 'What're you going to do when your kid Googles you?' are all questions that, even when

offered lightheartedly and in a spirit of ostensible support, feel less like genuine questions and more like a chastening. 'Remember, you're a MOM' and 'Remember, you have a mother' both mean 'Remember, you're a woman, and there are consequences.'

I told myself and my former student that I'd rather model sex positivity for my daughter than silence should she one day come across my essays. I get, as O'Connell does, that she might be teased for it in the future or that this will be the subject of her adult therapy sessions. But yeah, I think all of us who are writing about sex, love, and our bodies understand that there are consequences. We'd just like the conversation to change and for the questions to be about the work and not its effect on those we love. We're tired of being policed in this way.

I know that every time I publish an essay, I open myself up to judgment. Readers will decide all kinds of things about me that are true and not true. Future dates will read this. Some people will decide I date too much and that I'm a bad mom. Others will see that I'm just a woman who loves sex and connection and who believes mightily in the power of bodies to shape knowledge. If you are the latter, I hope you'll find me on Twitter and/or share your stories, too. But if you choose to stay silent, I understand. It's hard for women to tell the truth about dating, desire, and sex. We are usually punished for it. Sometimes the punishment is large-scale and public like Bette Midler scolding Kim Kardashian on Twitter for her nude selfie, but more often it's small-scale and knee-jerk: that tiny unexamined judgment, which disappears as quickly as ash, but leaves a residue.

Portals

Mostly, in my experience, Internet dating is fielding a lot of unwanted messages; sending a lot of messages that will be ignored; messaging back and forth to see if the person can finish sentences, has a sense of humor, and is not going to be a total dick; and discussing what your schedules are like, and when you may or may not meet up for a drink, coffee, or tea.

I remember when I first started online dating about three years ago, I told a more experienced friend, "I don't know, it's just, like, fun to get to meet new people and see what their lives are like." I don't remember her response, but I think it was a glassy-eyed stare over my shoulder. I bet she was thinking, "You stupid, stupid, girl," but she was sweet enough not to say that to me then.

What Internet dating is more than anything else is a time and energy suck. It takes energy to sift through profiles, write and respond to messages, and then go on first dates, which frankly, no matter how amazing, are still just an hour or two with a complete and total stranger. Because I am a mom, with a full-time teaching gig, several second jobs, and a lot of amazing friends, I often don't want to spend my energy in this way. I'd rather meet a friend for a drink or go to a yoga class than make small talk with a person I don't know. But I also still have hope, believe in love and connection, and find relationships appealing, and so I make deals with myself so that I don't quit altogether. I try to go on one date a week, I take dating apps off my phone so that I don't check out of boredom or habit, and sometimes I detox and shut down accounts.

Sometimes my married or coupled friends do this cute and exasperating thing of getting excited about my first dates. They say things like, "This could be the one!" or "I have a good feeling!" They seem to get that this is not an appropriate way of thinking about Internet dating or relationships with me (*The One? What is that?*), but what can they say? What do I say? *I'm meeting a stranger for a drink. Chances are we will not hit it off. I hope the person will not be mean or crazy. Because of the low odds of connection here, it's a good idea to think not at all of the future, to have zero fantasies and very low expectations.*

My therapist said recently that I'm tired. He's right. Maybe I'm a little jaded. Most men and women I talk to about Internet dating are confused by it. We do it because that's how you meet people. And it works. You do meet people. This essay is not a lament. I am not a Luddite. I have no desire to return to what dating was like in my twenties, when options consisted of picking someone up in a bar (though this has its occasional charms) and/or letting your friends fix you up.

I am interested in the solitary, voyeuristic online things we do that have no discernible outcome or pleasure but that increasingly orient our lives. What do we do alone, with our Internet portals? We fantasize and project. We inhabit the studium and we look for the punctum. We want to be pierced, wounded, and shot with an arrow. Most of us do anyway because it makes us feel alive, even if it hurts.

I just finished reading July Westhale's essay, "Loneliness and the Strange Alone-Togetherness of the Internet-Age" about her post-breakup Googling and how it functioned as a curative and a way to grieve. She writes, "the existence of information proves the existence of a thing: a dream, a wound, a love, a memory." I take this to mean that behind the random information we Google is something more real, something with feeling.

She echoes Barthes here, too; behind the image or the information is the wound. Behind the portal is eventually, perhaps, a person, made of flesh and blood, someone who we may or may not want to touch us. It's the possibility of connection—putting skin next to skin, looking someone in the eye, or the potential for intimacy that keeps us looking.

I wrote this essay to make a record, of sorts, of dating right now in my albeit very limited view. I haven't come across many essays about the nitty-gritty of Internet dating and none by a single, co-parenting mom in her forties, so I thought I'd write one. I also wrote this essay in solidarity with the other sex-positive women online and in podcasts who have told me about their dating lives. I love both the *Huffington Post* and *New York Magazine* sex podcasts. Maureen O'Connor of *New York* magazine is especially hilarious and smart when it comes to the realities of being single in New York right now.

I remain forever grateful to Alana Massey's funny and frank essay, "The Dickonomics of Tinder" for reminding me that I don't need to fall prey to the twisted little ideologies that tell women they should put up with all manner of bullshit to get laid and/or have a relationship. Her mantra, borrowed from lawyer and writer Laura

Holden, is, *Dick is abundant and of low value.*

I repeat this to myself so that I can leave a shitty first date quickly without feeling sad or sorry for the date because I was raised to be a good girl, kind and polite, in the face of boredom and narcissism. I say it out loud to my computer screen, when a guy I'm messaging on Tinder tries to order me to a mid-town street corner like I am take-out. Or when a 20-year-old writes to me on OkCupid that he likes to flash women and, "Would you like to see?"

Increasingly, after a first date, usually date two or three, when the date knows my full name, they Google me and find my very personal essays about my abusive father, my attempts at non-monogamy, eating, and my rare neurological disorder. As I wrote this essay, I wondered if this will be the final Google straw that breaks the camel's back and scares away all the dates. I suppose I didn't care because I kept writing.

I'm Here for the Time Killing

Internet dating is also an exceptionally good way to pass the time. Like all social media, it gives down time—the boredom, fear, loneliness, and distraction of it—a shape. It helps time function and gives it meaning. Not surprisingly, I am more interested in my dating apps when I am parenting because the hour-by-hour minutiae of being a single mom stretches and stops time like nothing else I've ever experienced. Are we really watching a fifth episode of *Jake and the Never Land Pirates?* Why, yes we are! *Are we still arguing over whether or not you go to bed at 8:30 or 9:00 at Daddy's house?* Seems like it!

This morning, my daughter woke up at 4 a.m. to barf. I was pleased with myself because I managed to catch the barf in a Tupperware bowl. She fell back asleep and I lay in bed wide awake for an hour or so before I said uncle and curled up in the covers closer to my kid, who still sometimes sleeps with me, and then I scrolled through my OkCupid matches. I had one reasonable message, another that was actually charming, and one from a 28-year-old.

My ex (the one from above that I met on OkCupid and fell into an exciting monogamous and then polyamorous relationship with for two years before deciding to just be friends) and I often talk about our online dating trends.

It's become one of our conversational set pieces because dating is too ridiculous and funny and stupid not to talk about. Or maybe it all just needs to be processed and said out loud or written down. I've always been a sharer, a teller, a blurter, and a huge talker. I tell my students and friends that to me there is no such thing as TMI. If I know you, I want to know your shit. Even if I don't know you, I kind of want to know your shit. I guess that's why I've taken to personal essays. Anything can be evidence if crafted well.

"I'm trending with 35-year-old working-class dudes who are native New Yorkers and men who have stomach ailments," I said to my ex at our favorite bar in Brooklyn.

"Ha," he laughed, and took a sip of the artisanal Old Fashioned that the bartender pretended to make just for us. "Working class like how?"

"Like heating and cooling, like warehouses," I said.

"Do you guys have stuff to talk about?"

"Music," I said. "What about you?"

"I'm trending with 50-year-old women from Connecticut who have just come out of a bitter divorce and would like for me to sexually awaken them," he said.

"You could do that," I said.

"But then what? What if I want someone to sexually awaken me?"

"You're already awake," I said and looked around the bar, which was reliably filled with men and women in their twenties and thirties, us, and the two 40-something year-old brothers who owned it.

"I know!" he said and we returned to our Old Fashioneds.

In "The Big Secret of Every Dating App: Tech Doesn't Matter," Maureen O'Connor writes, "But I have come to believe that the technology powering any one dating app doesn't matter at all. The only thing that matters is its users. In other words: It's not the technology, it's the marketing—and what kind of people that marketing attracts." O'Connor also reminds us that Internet dating does not mean that the sky is falling or that technology is going to change love and sex forever. It's just another thing we do to meet people, and we select our dating apps much like we select our favorite bars, cafes, and bookstores. Are there cute people there? Or is it full of sociopaths who won't stop staring at our faces? Do people speak to you there, or do they huddle up in a little weird secretive ball and hurl sexist one-liners at you? Is that dance floor truly queer, or does it just claim to be?

O'Connor is right and yet the volume and sheer amount of looking, cruising, staring, and studying we can do *has* changed. Never before in my life have I had access to so many images of people I may or may not want to date. Volume shifts attention. It can distract us. *Studium.* Or focus us. *Punctum.*

If you really want to know how each app functions, read Maureen O'Connor's essay. She's less grouchy about dating apps than I am, but here's my round-up, for what it's worth:

OkCupid: Like many users, I call this site Okstupid, or Okfineigiveup. It's like the stadium-size bar of dating apps. It has a lot of users, a *lot*, like maybe billions? I have met seriously nice, sexy, and smart people on this site who are cool and have jobs and passions and like to ask women questions about their lives and then mostly listen to the answers.

I have also received messages from people who write things like, "I notice your diminutive stature is at odds with your buxom (sic) and substantial bottom." *Hmmm…I haven't noticed that myself, but thanks. I will try not to trip over my own ass and boobs or let them fling the rest of my body dizzyingly up and down like a teeter-totter.* Or "Why haven't we had sex yet?!" In spite of this, I like the app and have returned to it after taking a break because there are a lot of people on it and so a lot of variety. Also, I read profiles. I like having that much information about someone and seeing whether or not they are funny in print. I don't like that anyone can message me. I think most of us women have to delete the majority of their messages, but maybe guys do, too?

Tinder: An addiction I once had that caught on like wild fire and nearly ruined my life. Ha. No seriously. In case you've been dead, this little app provides you with a pile of cards/profiles that you can swipe left (no!) or right (yes!) to.

If you both swipe right, it's a match, and you can begin the long-protracted messaging stage, which will most likely end in never meeting. It goes through your Facebook page (scary initially, and then not at all) to tell you if you have mutual friends or mutual friends of friends, which is nice because you can ask your friends about someone, although it's likely they won't know who the fuck you're talking about because most of us have too many Facebook friends.

I went on a couple of fun dates because of this app. It's cool that you can only message with people you've chosen, but it's a horrible time suck because it's too much like a video game. For the first month I had it, all I wanted to do with every free second was to swipe enough to match with someone and then keep swiping. The interface is also so addictive that it makes you want to swipe left and right in areas of your life where you can't. Bad work meeting. *Swipe.* My cat after he pees outside of the box. *Swipe.* The K-Mart at Astor Place. You get it.

Happn: I was obsessed with this app for the month I had it. The idea of it is cool. You can like people based on a little mosaic of profiles that pops up to let you know who you've crossed paths with after the fact. I think this is especially exciting for New Yorkers. There are so many of us! How will we find each other?

After you like a person, you can also send them a "charm" to let them know, and you can only message with someone if you both liked each other. It's fun in an anthropological way to know what cute people live near your subway stop or keep going to Gorilla coffee. I wanted this app to work, but I never got from messaging to an actual date with someone. I also had a couple of intense messaging experiences with people who just flat-out disappeared. Not that weird in the world of dating apps, but it seemed more pronounced for me on this site.

Bumble: Supposedly women-friendly. I only tried it for two days, and I don't remember it well. You both have to match to message each other, but the woman must initiate the contact. There are different rules for same-sex couples. I didn't stay on the app for long enough to figure out how it would work if I were writing to a woman.

I hated the timer. *I'm busy. Fuck off. I don't have to write to this guy in 24 hours!* That's what my brain said to my phone every time that timer started. Also, I'm not a big fan of passivity in men, so this app annoyed me.

Hinge: On this for about a month. Had one horrible date from it, and then shut it down out of irritation. It only allows you to see people who are in your Facebook network. In theory, this is safer? I found it boring and age-limiting. I love all of my Facebook friends, but I guess I'd rather go further afield for my dates. Apparently, according the CEO of Hinge who keeps flooding my inbox, they've revamped the site. I haven't gone back.

I'm curious about, but have never tried: Coffee Meets Bagel, The Grade, Match, and Taste Buds. I'm sure they'll be more apps soon because online dating is big business.

Community

On the first day of 2016, I went to the St. Marks Poetry Project New Year's Day Marathon benefit to read one of my poems to the audience. When I got up to the podium, I looked at my daughter, who promised to give me a thumbs-up when I finished, and then I forced myself to stare out at the 200 or more faces in the audience. I didn't linger for long enough because I was nervous, but I tried to see them all, to make a study of them, these great people who came to hear poetry on the first day of the new year.

Later, as I worked on the ending of this essay, I thought of the faces

I've been able to look at this year, both virtual and real. *How lucky you are to have access to so many portals and fantasies, spooling out like a ribbon in the wind*, I told myself, but I couldn't quite make it stick, and so later I wrote it down here in this essay. I wanted to remember this the next time someone I'd been messaging with disappeared with no explanation, or when I went on a shitty first date.

Perhaps I was trying to use these real audience faces—rapt and waiting for me to read to them—to steal myself for the more distant, far away faces in the portals. *These faces, both real and imagined, are a gift*. I wrote that down, too, so that I could carry it around with me, like a Zen koan or an aphorism or a good luck charm.

We all need our puzzles, and this one was mine.

OUR PRE-BORN CHILDREN

I read the email from my soon-to-be-ex-husband while I ate a spinach omelet. Ours was not a quick divorce. We were separated for three years before we signed up for a free mediation clinic. The mediator annoyed us by asking at the end of our first session if we were sure that we wanted to separate.

"You clearly have great affection for one another," he said. I stared at his red bowtie to staunch the tears.

"It's because we don't live together anymore," I managed. My ex glared at him. I could see a trace of the gruff masculinity I fell in love with. He looked like he might punch the guy.

I've joked with friends that it's easy to get a divorce when you have nothing to divide. We never owned an apartment together. Our used car died soon after we separated. We had $20,000 in credit card debt that we split down the middle. We're co-parenting equally and we teach in the same department and make the same barely livable by New York City standards salary, so there's no child or spousal support. I'm happy we never hired lawyers and got involved with the court system, which turn separation and divorce into a battle rather than another phase of a relationship. My ex and I were close friends again, which meant a lot to me as we raised our daughter together.

We had one thing left to decide. We'd had our daughter through IVF. She began as a twin pregnancy. The doctor implanted two embryos in me, and we froze the other two. As you know from previous essays, one of the babies died in the fourth month of the pregnancy. It was a grueling time. No doctor could explain what happened. I blamed myself. I decided it was the un-necessary amniocentesis or just my defective, useless body and then I hunkered down to try to get my daughter safely to the end of the pregnancy. She was born five months later. Beautiful. Red. Screaming and scrawny, like all babies in my family. She is, of course, the center of my world.

I never allowed myself to grieve the loss of that baby. It was not a child, but an embryo, I reasoned. I'd never met it or held it, and I never would. Just moments after my daughter slid out of me, my doctor showed me the clump of tissue that had once been that baby. I was high from the epidural, and the fact that my daughter was alive in the plastic basinet next to me. I looked at the mass, which resembled a giant red coin, and said, "Thank you for showing me that." I didn't know what else to say. I felt hysterically happy and tired and weird, my body squeezed out like an empty tube of oil paint. Cadmium red on the sheets and my hospital gown. I wasn't sure what my body was for anymore, now that I'd gotten a baby out of me alive.

That grieving I avoided burbled up and made the first year of my mothering scary and precarious. It didn't help that I couldn't breast-feed and that my daughter couldn't latch no matter what we did. I felt like a failure as a mother before I became a mother and all through that first year. These dark feelings added to the growing distance between my husband and me. In some way, I blamed him for the loss of that baby. None of it made sense.

I started therapy when my daughter was two and I learned to ease up on myself. My marriage fell apart and our separation was the right thing. Hard and sad, but better than living a lie.

The email was about a bunch of final bills we needed to separate—the phone bill, our daughter's college fund, life insurance, and the storage fee for the embryos. My ex wrote that he'd rather give the embryos to science because giving them to a couple for adoption wasn't something he was emotionally prepared to do. I understood why he felt that way. I sometimes felt that way, too. Other times, I envisioned an open adoption to a nice lesbian couple. In one fantasy version of this scenario, my daughter had siblings she could find in case she needed them to help her navigate her houseboat through the high waters of the impending climate apocalypse. In another, we all sometimes met up for a slightly boozy Thanksgiving. Kind of like the big gathering at the beginning and the end of Woody Allen's *Hannah and Her Sisters*, but with no Woody Allen, more lesbians, and children everywhere. Or maybe *The Kids Are All Right*, but with less sexual confusion. Mark Ruffalo would be there, of course.

When you do IVF, you sign a bunch of paperwork, and you agree that you understand your options for what to do with the frozen embryos. Depending on the state you live in, you can dispose of them, donate them to science, give them up for adoption, or keep them stored and frozen for as long as you want to pay for them. But when you sign that paperwork, you're not thinking about the future. You're definitely not imagining deciding what to do with your two frozen embryos once you've divorced your partner because all you want in that moment is a baby. You can't know that eight years later you'll be calling embryo adoption agencies and asking a lot of questions. You won't understand that embryo adoption is one of those strange little corners of the world where the religious right meets up with the liberal left to do business.

The first place I call openly identifies itself as a Christian organization on their website. They also refer to the embryos as "pre-born children," which gives my pro-choice heart a good, hard, thwack. The second place I call, is less overtly religious and refers to the embryos as just that. I have many questions for the incredibly nice women who answer the phones.

"Are all of the families you work with Christian?" I ask. *Because I would like my pre-born child to be raised by a bunch of atheist scientists please.*

"Can we have an open adoption?" *Because I would like to have more children, but I never will, so maybe this is some kind of weird, cosmic work-around in which I somehow get more kids and a sibling for my daughter.*

"Do you work with same-sex couples?" *Because right now, the only relationships I really believe in are the gay ones.*

"How do you deal with hereditary diseases?" *Because I have a rare neurological condition that if left undiagnosed is really quite awful, so I will need to consult with these parents.*

After each of these calls, I am no closer to making a decision. I realize that there is a part of me that is clinging to these embryos and what they mean—my future, the fantasy of a big family, and the possibility that there's more mothering in me. I also know the deep pain of infertility and I would like to give another struggling couple a chance at parenthood. While I am adamantly pro-choice and can't bear the Christian organization's calling those embryos "pre-born children," I realize I'm thinking of them that way. When you do IVF, they show you a photo of that little blast of cells they implant that will or will not become your kid. I first saw my daughter as that little cluster of cells. Now she is eight and she rides her skateboard through the apartment much to my yelling dismay. The cell-to-person journey is not lost on me. Have I fallen for this bit of pro-life propaganda? What does it mean that I'm calling a Christian organization that is willing to do me a great service and asking them not to be Christian?

I'd never been in such a privileged ethical quandary before. I knew how my ex felt. I talked it through with my therapist. I asked my closest friends. None of it helped.

Had I unconsciously decided that donating embryos to science is somehow morally lesser than giving them up for adoption. I believe in stem cell research, especially as someone who suffers from a neurological condition, so why couldn't I make this leap? I Googled stem cell research and embryo adoption, and I read that for many couples donating embryos to science is a middle ground—a way to give back when adoption doesn't seem quite right.

I also read about couples, who have good-bye ceremonies for the frozen embryos that they give up. Or that some practice what is called "compassionate transfer" by implanting them in the woman at a time when she cannot get pregnant. I didn't think I was up for such a transfer, but I liked the idea of a ceremony in which my ex and I said good-bye.

No matter what we decided, I knew that I needed to let go of the idea of a second child, my marriage, the ghost of that baby I lost, and the dream of a big, queer family that somehow comes together over time and distance because of adoption. But I am slow to let go, and I come late to my own feelings, especially grief.

How do we move into grief and loss instead of away from it? This movement is part of accepting my reality—what I have and what I failed to get. Saying good-bye to those embryos is also about accepting my own mortality, acknowledging that I am limited and there are certain ships that have sailed without me on deck.

On the day that I read that email from my ex, David Bowie passed away. Three months later, Prince died. After each death, I scanned my Facebook feed for all the status updates about these radical artists. They helped us envision new genders and alternative futures that were sex positive, fluid, kinky, and in color. Both were visionaries and shape shifters, who dressed for another better, funkier planet.

I thought of portals and cosmic exchanges. Since I don't believe in heaven, I Googled images of black holes and star clusters. I stared at my computer screen—where does the vortex of a worm hole lead? What are stars made of? Why are these images more comforting to me than any idea of an afterlife? I don't know. I'm more galactic than theistic. I'll pick Sun-Ra over church any day.

I imagine Prince and Bowie and those children I may never have as light in a shadowy world.

Not as pre-born, but rather as passing through.

THE FRAME

I went on what I then swore would be my last first internet date during winter storm Jonas. We'd been messaging on OkCupid and texting for about a week. He spoke Spanish, was a 50-year-old photographer, a native New Yorker, and seemed like he wouldn't try to murder me. That morning, I Facetimed with my kid, who was at her dad's apartment in Brooklyn and had just made a foot-high snowman out of wet snow, twigs, and carrots. I texted some of my married friends, who were snuggled up with their partners, watching Netflix and eating the fancy cheeses they had the foresight to buy before the storm. After that, I stared out the window of my seventh floor apartment, watched the snow fall sideways and panicked. The radio announced the subways would be closing at 4 pm. The sad single lady voice, which lived in certain parts of my head said, *You are totally alone. You are a shitty cook, who longs for someone to make you a good hot meal. Soon, you will be trapped in your apartment, where you will surely die of boredom and a lack of cheese.*

Hers was a voice I'd come to know well in the last three years since I separated from my husband. She loved to wake me up at 4 am with the whisper-question-hiss, *Where will you live when you get kicked out of your apartment?* When I gave a hungry homeless woman my peanut butter frosted brownie on the F platform at the West 4th Street station the other day, she shouted in my ear, *That's you someday if you don't come up with a plan.* In the waiting room of my therapist's office, she convinced me to read Suze Orman's financial advice column in *Oprah* and then berated me for not having done even one of the things Orman advises. *You're determined to live in New York City. Do you have to be a writer and a teacher? Couldn't you at least try to save for a down payment on something?*

"Meet at Corner Bistro at 2?" my phone chirped. It was the photographer.

"Yes!" I texted back instantly just to shut up that voice on my head.

I bundled up and made my way out into the afternoon beauty of the snowstorm. As my boot hit the first snow pile, something child-like came over me, and I broke into a little run, dance, jig that lasted a full block. I took pictures of New Yorkers carrying cases of beer down the middle of Seventh Avenue and kids playing hockey on Jane Street and posted them to Facebook. I waited for the likes to roll in. My face and phone were wet with snow. As I approached the bar, I had the rom-com-like thought that accompanies even the most jaded of single women—that if I like the guy, this would be a cool, funny story about how we first met. *We braved the blizzard! I just had a feeling!*

When I got there, he was busy looking at a woman about fifteen years younger than me who fit my description of having a punk, pixie haircut and was wearing overalls.

"I thought that was you," he said. "Because you said you like over-alls in your profile."

"When I was 21," I clarified.

He recovered from that disappointment and we found a booth in the back. We ordered cheeseburgers and whiskey and settled into the stop and start that is the hallmark of internet first date conversations. He told me about living in Japan for five years. He asked me questions about my life. He had a smattering of freckles along his nose that I decided were cute. I liked his wavy hair. He apologized about the other woman and said, "I like you."

"This is nice," I said and meant it. I was happy to be out of my apartment and to have some company.

He ordered us a second round of whiskeys.

"Are you worried about the trains?" I asked.

"Nah," he said. "Governor Cuomo said that it's your citizen's duty to give shelter to anyone stranded in the storm."

I laughed nervously. He downed the second whiskey and ordered a beer and another whiskey. I finished my burger and dipped my fries into the mayonnaise. I knew this was my hot meal for the day.

The date spiraled into badness the way many first dates do. Nothing terrible, just the grim realities of New York lives. He raised his fists in triumph when I told him I had a Ph.D. and shouted, "I'm moving up the world!" After that, he admitted he'd been sleeping on his sister's couch for the last five years and had no plans for finding his own place or even a share. He told me he didn't work much anymore and how hard it was to be an artist. I agreed and ordered myself another shot. I had great sympathy for him, and still I knew this was not a guy I could date again. I'd taken care of plenty of men. It my twenties and in my marriage, I'd too often turned into the mom, the one in charge, who had all the ideas about the future and who was no fun compared to my cool, in-the-moment-partner. This role got old.

I'm interested in partnership, sure, but I want the guys I date to at least have beds. *He wants a mommy,* I thought, and then his phone rang.

"Hold on," he said raising his finger at me. "It's my mother."

He took the call and spoke to her for about five minutes. I downed my shot.

When he hung up, I thanked him for meeting, gave him a limp hug, and made my way back out into the snow. On the walk back to my apartment, I watched young couples help each other through the snow banks and I felt a little sorry for myself. Still, when I made it back to my apartment, I felt relieved. Happy to be alone, instead of making awkward small talk with a stranger in a bar.

The next day I shut down my OkCupid account. I said Uncle. That date was the last one is a series of bad ones. People who lied about their ages and where they lived. A man who made fun of me for not having tenure, and then admitted he was currently unemployed. Another photographer who misrepresented himself so wildly in his profile pictures that I couldn't find him at the bar where we met. A guy who didn't have much to say, except, "You're pretty." One who talked for an hour straight without asking me a single question about myself and then wondered why I left. A man I never met but messaged for a month who I began to suspect was pretending he lived in New York but was really in London. Nothing shocking. Nothing that different from what most of my single friends have experienced. I've had good experiences, too. A man I fell in love with and dated for a year, who is now one of my closest friends. Sweet, divorced dads who were fun to commiserate with about kid barf and our exes' antics. Some hot flings.

I didn't miss the anxiety of Internet dating—the obsessive checking of my messages to see who has responded or not, the messages from people in other countries or from soldiers at faraway military bases that read only ever, "Hi, wanna chat?", the couples who wrote to me because they wanted a unicorn—a single woman who is open to swingers—and see in me something butch and femme, and the constant back and forth that may or may not lead to a supremely mediocre experience.

I wonder how many of us feel addicted to these sites? OkCupid, Tinder, and Happn can heighten the sense of free-floating anxiety and distraction we already feel from texting and social media because of the added promise of romantic and sexual connection. My two months on Tinder resulted in just two dates. I spent hours swiping and trying to get more matches. It was addictive, and fun, and not at all real. The GPS of Happn sent me scurrying to different far-flung neighborhoods to up my potential crushes. OkCupid allows you to see who visits you, heightening the feeling of always being surveilled.

The withdrawal was intense. I trained myself to accept that there is nothing romantic going on in the world of my phone. My life without Internet dating was calmer, yes, but also a bit dull. As Valentine's Day came and went, I wondered how many of us were using these apps to assuage the anxiety and sadness that comes from being single on a holiday steeped in the ideology of coupledom.

On weekends, I was tempted to reactivate my OkCupid account. I like love and I'm interested in partnership. I was also increasingly happy on my own. Would I choose boredom or anxiety? Celibacy or dating? Do I always have to make everything so black and white?

One Saturday morning, I woke up and walked outside to get a bacon, egg, and cheese sandwich from the corner bodega. My breakfast treat for the week. I texted a guy I'd dated a couple of months ago to say hello. He texted back that he'd moved back in with his girlfriend of nine years but that he'd been thinking about me. It was a nice exchange. He'd been kind and fun, but we hadn't really connected. I wished him luck. He told me to text if I ever wanted to get coffee. I wasn't sure why I reached out. Boredom. Longing. The sky was blue and it was 50 degrees. Warmth. Possibility. Sun on my animal face.

I came back into my apartment to write. I took a break to read an essay on female friendship by Sophie Lucido Johnson, "A More Perfect Love," which was punctuated by Johnson's own beautiful blue and black watercolors. A close friend and I had recently had a toxic fight. It felt like a break-up. She wanted things from me I couldn't give her. I felt bullied and I lashed out. I regretted my anger. I knew I would, and yet our relationship felt off to me, beyond repair. My kid was with her father and I missed her. Johnson charts the complicated romantic friendships women sometimes have with other women and her deep love for her best friend Hannah. She wonders, too, about the idea of the soul mate and our cultural belief that our spouse will become our "best friend," thereby replacing all the best friends that came before. She eventually moved away from Hannah, explored various configurations of polyamory, and then moved in with a boyfriend. She admits, "No one was everything to me all at once, and it took me years to realize that that was okay," and then wonders, "Aren't there relationships that fall somewhere between platonic and non-platonic? Isn't there love that exists beyond "friendship" and outside of "lover" and paradoxically both inside and outside of "family?"

I found the essay deeply comforting. It kept me from re-activating my OkCupid account and for that alone I was grateful, not because I won't at some point. I just needed to settle into that break and to explore the ways in which my friendships and my relationship with myself (as cheesy as that might sound) could be platonic, romantic, and sustaining.

What I found less anxiety inducing than dating was the notion of a network of friends. A community. A net that catches me, but that doesn't trap me. I don't want one best friend, but I am lucky enough to have many deep friendships that at times can feel romantic. The friend who cooks for me. The friend who gets me high and makes me laugh so hard that I feel joy. The friend who takes me dancing and screams the lyrics to Miley Cyrus songs with me. The friend who understands when I'm depressed and can't leave the house. The friend who loves my daughter as much as she loves me. The new friends, who were once my students. The friend I've known since we were sixteen.

Some of my fantasies for the future involve shared housing with close friends—a brownstone we somehow carve up into apartments, a cabin in the woods where we meet on the weekends, or a writer's colony-like campground where we each have our own little bungalow and meet for communal meals. A few years ago, I watched a documentary called *Happy* and I learned about co-housing, which is new to the U.S., but has a long tradition in Denmark and Sweden. My fantasies fit with the idealism of co-housing movements—bonds that are not about marriage and monogamy, but about community and collaboration.

Around the same time I was on my internet dating break, Rebecca Traister published an essay "The Single American Woman" in *New York* magazine about the voting power and history of single women in America. Not surprisingly, there's more than us than ever, and we're making our demands more clear—a livable minimum wage, paid family and sick leave, and access to reproductive services to name a few. Her statistics are particularly illuminating:

> In 2009, the proportion of American women who were married dropped below 50 percent. In other words, for the first time in American history, single women (including those who were never married, widowed, divorced, or separated) outnumbered married women. Perhaps even more strikingly, the number of adults younger than 34 who had never married was up to 46 percent, rising 12 percentage points in less than a decade. For women under 30, the likelihood of being married has become

astonishingly small: Today, only around 20 percent of Americans are wed by age 29, compared to the nearly 60 percent in 1960.

I wondered why if unmarried women outnumber married women, I often feel surrounded by couples? If there's so many of us, where are we all hiding? Why aren't we hanging out more? And why is it so hard for me to conjure up an image of solitary, strong, single women from my childhood archive of T.V. shows, literary figures, and cartoon characters?

I squint really hard as I type and tried to call one forth. I see Georgia O'Keefe standing in the desert underneath a blue dome of sky. Wonder Woman pops up to block some bullets with her magical silver bracelet cuff shields. I flash on Angela Davis, fist in the air as she stepped into a California courtroom to face the phony charges leveled against her by the state of California. I am happy to see these women.

Still I want more for myself and for my daughter. I'm tired of rom coms and marriage plots. I want more stories about women who go it alone, who have sex and love in their lives, but are not consumed by the quest for a husband. I want movies about "alternative kinship structures," as my friend, the playwright Madeleine George wrote in her play, *Seven Homeless Mammoths Wander New England*. I want essays, novels, and poems about sex-positive queer and straight women, who do it their own way, and give way less fucks about married people. I want people to stop asking me if I'm seeing anyone and to quit reassuring me when I say I'm not.

Just work on your self, and then someone will come. It happens when you least expect it. It will surprise you, but that person is out there.

"What if they're not?" I sometimes say back.

"Who cares?" I shrug at them.

I want a plot that meanders and a protagonist who has no idea where she's going and doesn't really care.

I don't believe in saviors, princes, or heroes.

I like it when the sun is so bright on my face I have to squint. It was the end of February. Soon, it would be spring, and then summer.

I'll wade around in a fountain filled with children and homeless teenagers and I'll remember that I'm not just a brain in a jar, a writer and a teacher, who, like all of us, has too many jobs. I'm an animal, too. I'll sweat in my cut-off shorts and tank top and my sunglasses will slide down my nose. I will be mistaken for other kinds of women or I will be invisible. A tourist will accidentally include me in the frame of her picture. My daughter will splash me and I will splash back. Later, the tourist will wonder who I am, and then she will crop me out of her nearly perfect photo of the Washington Square Park arch.

No matter. I exist. Regardless of whether I'm in the frame or outside of it.

THE THREAD

1

Sometime during my senior year of high school, my mother went on a laundry strike. Her goal, as I understood it, was to get my father to pick his underwear up off the bathroom floor, carry them to the hamper, and eventually wash them. She made my brother and I promise not to help him.

At the time, I naively thought this activist intervention would work. Strike! It was simple and direct. My father, like many fathers of that baby boomer generation, made double what my mother made and did very little if any housework. He occasionally mowed the lawn and shoveled the snow, but mostly my brother did those chores for his allowance.

The fact that this was the mode of problem solving between my parents says a lot about the state of their marriage. Did my mother see herself as a worker at my father's company, our family? Had negotiations broken down so totally that striking was my mother's only option? I had stopped talking at the dinner table though, at the time, I thought of it less as a form of protest than as a coping mechanism. At night, my brother drank beer on the deck and threw the empty cans into the yard. After the snow melted in the spring, the muddy grass revealed cases worth of them. Maybe we were all just biding our time—striking, drinking, or not talking until we could get out.

The strike was a failure. My father held out for longer than any of us could have imagined. When he ran out of clean underwear he drove to the mall and bought several packages of new Fruit of the Looms. The dirty underwear piled up so high behind the bathroom door that we couldn't open it. My father never acknowledged the strike and he never complained about his dirty underwear. He simply refused to wash them.

My mother eventually gave in. I remember her standing in front of the mouth of the washing machine, stuffing his underwear into it. "There's something wrong with your father."

I'm sure I agreed. In the war that was my parents' marriage I'd taken my mother's side, and like the second-wave feminist she'd raised me to be, I decided that our problems with my father were both personal and political.

My mother always worked. We had babysitters and went to daycare. After school we had more babysitters, until middle school, when we stayed home by ourselves. For years, she was a secretary. She practiced for typing tests, took shorthand, and disliked most of her bosses but bore it in the way that all secretaries and assistants must. After that, she became a job counselor for the state of New York, which led to a position in our local Boys Club. Once there, she was eventually promoted to Assistant Executive Director then Executive Director positions. Once she became the Executive Director, she was one of a handful of female directors nationally. When she returned from the yearly national conferences for the Boys Clubs of America, which would later become the Boys and Girls Clubs of America, she spoke of the insults she had to endure from the male directors who ignored her and/or didn't believe she could be a director. She, too, was sometimes surprised by her position. She had an associate's degree, and spent several years working on her BA through Empire State College before realizing she didn't care enough to complete it.

During a brief six-month period of unemployment just before she was hired at the Boys Club, my brother and I begged her to stop working altogether. We longed for a mom who made cookies and picked us up after school, and we were total jerks about it. For those six months, she walked us dutifully back and forth to school, tried out new brownie recipes, and finished a complicated needlepoint project. Then she found a job at the place that would employ her for the rest of her working life.

The women in my family have always worked. It was an economic necessity and a way to have freedom from the largely shitty choices they made in marriage. Your own job meant your husband had less control over you. Your own money meant a small degree of freedom in marriage. A job meant you could leave the house and have your own friends. It was an antidote to boredom. A vocation shaped your sense of self.

My grandmother survived her marriage to an abusive second husband because she worked at the post office. She described taking the civil service exam and getting the top score as one of the proudest moments of her life. When she started working at her tiny town's post office, she said of her husband, my step-grandfather, "What could he say? I was bringing home a paycheck."

My grandmother should have left him, but since she couldn't bring herself to do that she got a job instead. My mother should have left my father much sooner into their almost 20-year marriage. They probably never should have gotten married. They were both 24. In 1970, that was late to marry. My mother has admitted to me that she cried on her wedding day. Not tears of joy.

My mother and I don't always agree on what it's like to be a single, divorced woman. I get lonely sometimes and I miss having a partner, but I like my freedom and am determined more than ever to take care of my daughter and myself. I don't ever want to be dependent on a man again. For me, it's a feminist issue.

I know, too, that there is something hard and broken in this stance. I am afraid to depend on anyone, especially a man I love. Anyone who knows me well understands that some of this stance is because of my father, who has been emotionally, and, when we were children, sometimes physically abusive. My therapist would remind me that everyone needs to attach, and he'd be right. But how to attach without dependency? How to love like an adult and not a little girl? How to believe in men when your father was, and has remained, wholly unbelievable in his actions toward his children? What if you love men dearly but find them somewhat lacking in the stepping-up department? Sometimes my therapist annoys me by telling me that he believes there are good men out there for me and that he wants me to believe, too. He says this not because he believes that I need a man but because all humans have attachment needs. Still, I find this

Disneyfication of the "good man" objectionable. Are they like Tinker Bell and her fairy crew? If I believe enough, will one appear? Sometimes I don't even want a man but a woman, or someone who, like me, is less interested in gender binaries.

My mother, who is now married to another man, struggles, like all married couples do, and is fearful about the future. I don't think her fears are real (she owns her home outright, is on Social Security, and has a small pension), but I must acknowledge them as real to her. Losing her house. Living alone. Dying alone.

In America right now—with its shitty social welfare policy, lack of family leave, patched-together health-care system, and a party in power that actively works on policies that punish and destroy poor people—it's pretty hard to not be afraid. I know of a couple of women who stay married because they don't believe that financially they can make it on their own in this country. They might be right. According to a 2014 CNN Money article by Melanie Hicken, "On average, women 65 years and older rely on a median income of around $16,000 a year—roughly $11,000 less than men of the same age, according to a Congressional analysis of Census data. And many elderly women rely exclusively on Social Security benefits."

At this stage in my grand plan for female autonomy and emancipation, I still live paycheck to paycheck, have no plans for future housing, and no savings whatsoever (for myself, or for my daughter to go to college). I own no property, nor do I have money for a down payment on anything. I also know that I'm lucky—to have housing, to send my daughter to a good public school, and to be able to pay most of my bills. Still, like most Americans, I have my get-rich-quick schemes. I'll sell my novel for six figures! Then, once I sell that novel, I'll be able to leave my long-term contract faculty job and get a tenured position somewhere! My father—who, according to my brother, is hoarding a cool million—and I will patch things up and he'll leave me an inheritance! One day, I'll meet someone and fall in love again and we'll decide to live together, and he or she will be rich and generous!

These last two are particularly vexing fantasies for me because they rely on the idea of a savior, and so lately I try to resist them. I don't want to be saved anymore. That was a girlhood ideology that slunk into most of my adult life. I suspect I'm not the only woman in the world who has fallen for this one. We can't be too hard on ourselves for falling for ideology. Ideology works because it's unconscious. It's a thread we can use to hold together the fabric of our thoughts.

2

Though my relationship with my mother is a complicated one, she has given me many gifts. She taught me to work and to scheme and to dream. In the early '70s, my mother and her best friend S formed the local chapter of the National Organization for Women in our small upstate New York town. Several years later, my brother and I, along with S's two sons, waved them off as they drove to Chicago to march for the Equal Rights Amendment. I remember how defeated they were when it didn't pass.

The background noise of much of my childhood was listening in on their schemes. There was something zany about them when they were together. They had endless ideas, they gossiped, and they made each other laugh. We, the children, were in their orbit. Or we were upstairs beating the shit out of each other.

There was a draft of a feminist cookbook for husbands who didn't know how to cook and a store S opened called Cheese and Crafters that sold local cheeses, croissants, and handmade crafts. The store folded after a year, not long after we kids ate our weight in cheese curds. My mother and S had long talks in the kitchen about the sewing projects they were working on, how to get a better job, and how to change their husbands.

But first there was the NOW chapter, which my mother claims to have grown bored with when someone brought in mirrors so that they could examine their vaginas. "Not for me," my mother shrugged when she told me this story, a faint look of disgust on her face. She said the same thing recently when I told her to start watching *Broad*

City. I am often unsure which kinds of sexual things will disgust my mother. I guess Ilana, my favorite character on *Broad City* and pretty much any television show ever, is, in her own way, the modern-day equivalent to the 1970s group vaginal self-examination. Ilana is, after all, all about the pussy.

From my mother and S I learned that feminism is a dream for the future, a fantasy you talk about but never quite grasp. I wonder if many third-wave daughters of second-wave mothers think this. Or maybe many activists and feminists in particular feel this way because change is slow, and our government is woefully behind in providing the things the majority of feminists and liberals in this country want: affordable birth control and access to abortions, paid parental leave, a $15 minimum wage, and stricter gun control, to name a few.

In college, I read the work of black, brown, and queer feminists, and I learned that feminism was about making your own path, building utopian spaces, and exploring a deeply exciting, witchy sexuality. I tripped out on Gloria Anzaldúa's idea of "la conciencia de la Mestiza" (the mestiza consciousness). I went to a Bikini Kill concert in London when I was studying abroad in Madrid and felt the thrill of being invited to the front of the hall. I left the man I was with in the back, and he complained afterward that it wasn't fair. I didn't care. In graduate school I read bell hooks's *Teaching to Transgress*, I started consulting for Bard College's Institute for Writing and Thinking, and I began to work toward creating an inclusive, democratic classroom, where everyone could work and play together. The child psychologist and grandfather of play theory, D. W. Winnicott, calls it "serious play."

In my favorite course, I taught this academic year, Youth in Revolt: Case Studies in Global Activism, we studied subculture theory and style as a system of readable signs, and then we delved into the Weather Underground, the Black Panther Party, Tiananmen Square, riot grrrl, Tahrir Square, and Pussy Riot. One day I made a riot grrrl playlist and we listened to it while making zines about the things in our lives that piss us off and wanted to change. The class before, we'd read Sara Marcus's history of the riot grrrl movement, *Girls to the*

Front, and Jack Halberstam's *Gaga Feminism*. The theory and history of zines and DIY movements underpinned our making of a tangible object. As Bratmobile and Heavens to Betsy and Junglpussy (I decided she's a latter-day riot grrrl/hip hop) screamed and groaned in the background, we wrote, sketched, and collaged. Inside the zine were our stories about the world and ourselves.

From this class, and these students in particular, I learned I prefer a messy, improvisational feminism, where the theory and history sit comfortably underneath or alongside the making and doing and become the background chatter and noise to our lives: writing, art making, cooking, sewing, fucking, and taking care of children and friends. What makes me happiest in the classroom is when we manage that kitchen-table feeling I saw in my mother and S when I was a little girl. Politics, love, laughter, sadness, and schemes—all stewing together on the stove top.

Perhaps this is why I'm drawn to photographer Carrie Mae Weems's groundbreaking "Kitchen Table Series" (1990). In these black-and-white photographs, the kitchen, and more specifically Weems and her own kitchen table, center the frame. Children, lovers, and friends revolve around the table, but the constant is the woman, who, according to Weems, claims the domestic space as political, not just for African American women, but for all women.

I left for college the same year that Weems released these photographs, desperate to escape the domestic cage of my parents' disintegrating marriage, convinced the only way to be political was to march in the streets and to sit and stand in solidarity at rallies and protests.

3

If I could get one of those cosmic work-arounds that we all sometimes crave and go back in time, I'd fire up my flux capacitor, zip back to the mid-'80s, and ask my parents to redo their divorce.

My big joke about my parents' divorce is that they started talking about it when I was 10, but didn't make it stick until I was 18. Ha.

"I'm divorcing your father," I remember my mother saying to me as she cried on her bed after a particularly horrible argument. She was making a pro and con list on a yellow legal pad for whether she should stay or go. Like the copies of *Penthouse*, *Playboy*, and *Hustler* my father kept on the coffee table, she left it out on the nightstand. Later, I read it. I was 14 or 15. I don't know if my brother saw it. I don't know where my brother was, probably in his room, re-working the elaborate system of ropes and pulleys he'd rigged to make it impenetrable. His closet was attached to the crawl space, which he'd made into a lair for playing video games and sneaking beers. These were our early roles. I was over-involved and he was hiding.

"I am the enemy of this family," my father said around the same time, in the middle of a typically gray and freezing upstate New York winter. We'd all been fighting about something—maybe it was what to order for delivery. My mom had stopped cooking out of sheer exhaustion, but we could never agree about what local fast-food fare to order because for this one moment of every day, we were each determined to have our desires met and dug in.

"I want a cheeseburger and baked potato from Wendy's." "I want Taco Hut." "I want chicken nuggets from McDonald's."

"I am the enemy of this family," he possibly repeated. Perhaps my mother gave him one of her withering looks. I can't remember. Their fights bled together, and like many unhappily married couples, they had the same fight over and over again. I heard them so often they felt scripted. *Now's the part where mom says she can't take it anymore. Here's the part where dad says fuck off.*

My father stood up. He was crying. He did that sometimes. Usually after he'd done something particularly mean, and he felt guilty about it. "It's really hard to have your father die and your family hate you," he shouted back at us as he slammed the front door. We listened to the garage door open and his car drive down the snowy street.

I'm not sure what the rest of us did. We probably talked about him behind his back. Or ordered the food we wanted. I know I felt an impossible sadness and rage in my stomach. I wanted to comfort him because I had no idea what it felt like for your father to die, but

I knew it must be horrible. But if his own father beat him, wasn't he glad he was dead? I knew from eavesdropping on rare phone calls and from the stories my father told about his childhood that their relationship was distant and brutal.

I felt sorry for my dad. I loved him. I hated him. I had occasionally wished him dead. Mostly, I wanted him to be a better dad, more like the TV dads I was obsessed with—Pa from *Little House on the Prairie* or Dr. Huxtable from *The Cosby Show*. But I needed my mother more because she took better care of me, so I sided with her, not understanding until I was much older and in therapy that my brother and I should never have been involved in the drama of their marriage.

One day, the August before I went away to college, my father and I were both packing. I have an image of him putting some of his books in a box while standing in his office. He is surrounded by his guitars, his most cherished possessions. I am walking to the bathroom, which is just past his office. I am ignoring him. I say nothing, I make no eye contact, but I see that he is moving slowly, as if underwater. Each book, each object is an opportunity for contemplation, for staying put, and for going slow. My father is the master of passive resistance.

That summer before college I was completely off the rails. My first boyfriend, the love of my 18-year-old life, dumped me for a blonde who called herself a performance artist. This was too much for me to bear, so I started sleeping with an alcoholic football player from the next town over, who was occasionally so drunk he fell asleep on top of me. I went to his house whenever I could and a couple of times I sniffed poppers with him, his sister, and his best friend. To do this day I recall those afternoons of sniffing poppers as some of the best of my life. Pure pleasure. Bliss. Giggling until I fell off the bed. I was kind of in love with his sister, but I told no one. Instead, I made out with the best friend in my mother's car in the woods. One of my closest old friends, who had spent the year mostly not talking to me, came back into my life, and told me she'd been in a cult and had to get deprogrammed by experts who showed her videos of Hitler youth and refused her a shower until she would listen. I was ecstatic to have her back. I'd missed her so much, but I was also confused. I didn't know how to process what had happened to her. Another close friend decided not to go away to college as planned. I thought this was a big mistake, but I didn't say so. I felt betrayed in our pact to get out of our small town, no matter what.

That summer I was also doing a lot of acid. I came home tripping one night to find my father awake and chatty in the family room. I tried to sneak past so that I could hide in my room and stare at myself in the mirror until the acid wore off.

"Sit with me?" he asked.

I nodded yes and kept my head down, afraid that my father would see my giant dilated pupils. I was carrying a tub of French onion dip and a bag of chips, which I wasn't sure I could eat in my fucked-up state but was determined to have in my room.

The room was dark, the TV on, to what I don't know. My father was saying things, but I didn't quite understand what they were, so I said yes and murmured a lot. My father hates interruptions, so this usually works just fine. Or maybe we talked about something real. Maybe I managed to have a conversation with him. I can't remember. I tried to eat the chips and dip, but the texture was all wrong and felt thick and heavy on my tripping tongue. I couldn't swallow.

In the flux-capacitor version of this story, I tell him I'm tripping and that I started taking acid after he gave me Tom Wolfe's *The Electric Kool-Aid Acid Test*. I want him to understand that part of my dream for my own future is to become like the Merry Pranksters but without the complicated sexual politics. Maybe I tell him that I love him and that I hate him and that these feelings I have for him are the strongest feelings of my life so far. I demand that he grow up and move on and move out and start a new life because that's what I plan to do, and in my 18-year-old righteousness, I cannot understand why my parents won't do the same. I cannot bear their lingering. Their slow pace. Their endless marriage. But I can't go back. I said none of this. I had no language. This is why I took acid. To become more fully the mute, stupid animal I longed to and imagined myself to be.

I see now that this conversation is the blueprint for many of our future conversations. My father saying a lot and me saying very little until I can escape. His monologues. My silence. This is the arrangement he prefers because when I talk, I confuse him. I don't make sense. He says I mumble. He says I am purposely difficult and that I enjoy it.

Now that I have gone through my own divorce and separation, I can better appreciate what a radical re-alignment it is—the self must be re-worked. The first year of separation is vastly different from the fourth year when you sign the divorce papers. I want to forgive my parents for their messy '80s divorce. I want to say it went down like many divorces of that era. I'm glad, too, that the children of these messy divorces, my brother and myself included, are trying to do it differently. More co-parenting. Less litigation. More therapy.

Still, my parents' divorce is the wound that has marked us all. I missed the mother I had before my parents split; in some ways, she felt more together. She knew who her enemy was, at least. It was even harder to get to know the man who is my father. My mother tried to protect us from him. She'd been a shield. Now I had to face him alone. Once I'd gone to graduate school, my mother slid into a deep depression. She'd escaped my father, but there were still problems. She wanted a partner. Dating in my small town was no picnic. I remember her sad phone calls and my trips home when she would spend big chunks of time after work and on weekends in bed. Her work kept her grounded then. She felt needed there.

I wonder about the work we do to shape our lives—for money, on the self, with our friends, lovers, and children.

Working through. A work-around. Work it. Get to work. All work and no play. You need to work on your shit. Busy work. Work it out. Dirty work. A nasty piece of work. Piecework. Women's work.

4

Lately, as one of the many metaphorical possibilities I offer my students for thinking about the structure of essays, I tell them that the essay is a quilt. I'm stealing this from my dear graduate school mentor, Darlene Forrest, who taught me some of the smartest and best things I know about teaching, learning, and writing.

Sometimes, when I'm writing, I pull the thread and the essay unravels. Mostly, if I try hard enough, I can stitch the pieces together and find the thread. Essays are the only sewing I do these days.

I worry that I'll make a shoddy quilt. My mother is a precision quilter. I'm in awe of the small bits of math, the piecing and the patterns that go into even a small quilt. My daughter and I each have quilts she made us hanging in our rooms.

I remember an exhibition of the Gee's Bend quilters I saw in my late 20s at a museum. These quilts, made by African American women (many of them descendants of slaves) starting in the 1920s in Alabama, are improvisational and in a style the women call "my way." Made from old clothes and blankets and leftover Sears, Roebuck corduroy, these quilts are riffs on patterns that subvert the very idea of patterns and precision. They take flight into their own design and iteration, and they are the most beautiful quilts I've ever seen.

When I was in elementary school, I was in 4-H. I sewed and quilted. I made a small wooden bench for my dolls, my initials stenciled on it, from a kit. I won a ribbon after walking down a runway made out of hay bales in a pleated sleeveless drop-waist dress I'd sewn. In my 20s and 30s, my sewing skills turned me into the unofficial tailor for my friends and husband. I found sewing dull—I don't know why—and the garment I envisioned was never what I wound up making. Mending was even more tedious. But I quit sewing because I couldn't bear the seam ripper—that little tool with the hook claw that rips out the thread. I couldn't stand to admit that I made such a mistake, one that has to be entirely undone. I remember my mother saying, "Looks like you might have to rip it out," and my dismay at those words. But, sometimes, the garment is too messed up. You have to accept that, start over, and make new stitches over the holes of the previous ones.

My mother often ripped the seams out for me because she knew I found it tedious and depressing. Then, she'd help me thread the needle of the sewing machine and we'd start again.

RESISTANCE DANCE

Sorry

When Seth and I got to *Bedlam* it was more crowded than usual—full of bankers in button-down shirts and young women with long hair in short black dresses and heels. We pushed through the crowd. One of those women tapped Seth on the shoulder.

"Go back and apologize to my boyfriend," she slurred.

"Why?" I interrupted.

"Okay." Seth shrugged.

"But why?" I pressed.

"He didn't say excuse me." She fell drunkenly into us.

"You are *so* pretty," Seth said. Total sincerity. Total shade.

She smiled and pulled Seth towards a circle of banker bros while I sat in a booth and watched people funnel out the door. I thought my 44 year-old-woman thoughts. *You're older than everyone here. You can only pass for so long,* and then I stopped. *Everyone is entitled to dance.*

"What did he say to you?" I asked when Seth came back, balancing a whiskey and two beers.

"We'll share the second beer!" he shouted as we toasted. My heart swelled with love for him—my former student and now a friend, a poet and media studies scholar who liked to go out dancing with me.

"He didn't even know I'd bumped into him."

"That girl." I rolled my eyes.

An hour later, after most of the wealth had left the bar, we screamed the lyrics to Justin Beiber's "Sorry" in the middle of the dance floor. Now it was just us: queer men and women and their sort of straight girlfriends—a lot of folks who would fit under the hashtag #neverthelessshepersisted.

Sometimes the D.J. stopped the song, so it was just our voices, the dancers, shouting lyrics which meant a lot to each of us in that drunken moment.

Dance floors have staying power: they mutate and shift depending on the dancers, the music, the DJ; they endlessly re-invent themselves. They pop up, go underground, happen by accident, are weekly, bi-weekly, and once a month. They exist at protests, in warehouses, in bars with back rooms, in bars with no space, in tiny apartment parties, or whenever friends get ready to go out. Like many of the people who choose to dance, they persist.

Hey Ya!

In the middle of Dodie Bellamy's essay "The Beating of Our Hearts" in her amazing collection *When the Sick Rule the World*, I found my friend, the poet David Buuck, and the question of how poets and writers navigate activist spaces. In my favorite section, Bellamy recounts a party full of Occupy Oakland activists. The dance floor erupted when Tiffany's version of "I Think We're Alone Now" came on:

A group of poets hurled selves across the living room and began a spontaneous freeform dance, writhing and flailing together in a frenzy,…ape[ing] dramatic Modern Dance moves, confronting and spinning one another in Bob Fosse meets apache meets punk maneuvers that were at once stagy, awkward, and sexy. The conversation stopped. Those of us who weren't dancing, witnessed. (170)

I've been part of similar dance parties. Poets and teachers, whose day-to-day work is in the caring and helping industries. We teach. We do social justice work. We volunteer. We parent. Sometimes we lose track of our bodies and then we reclaim them in fits of spontaneous dancing that to outsiders looks mesmerizing and startling.

Who are those sexy nerds? Why are they so joylessly unhinged? Who knew she could move her ass that way? What's he doing over there in the corner?

Some of my wildest dancing has been with teachers, poets, and artists during the summer at an intensive summer writing program for incoming freshmen at Bard College. It was where I first met David, who probably introduced me to Dodie Bellamy's work. The days were long and sometimes the students were entitled, but mostly they were wild nerds who experimented with whatever radical pedagogies we unleashed on them with great enthusiasm. Still, we were exhausted and underpaid, living on campus in dorm rooms that made us feel simultaneously infantilized and frat-house free.

When we let loose, we really let loose. We took over the porches and common areas. We did shots out of flasks in the woods. We stood on tables and grinded up against each other. We had fights with squirt guns that ended in dancing and crab-walk races. Once, a small group of us streaked through an open field while a larger group watched. Occasionally our students looked on as we danced our wild dances on the porch. We didn't care. One or two asked if they could join us. Sometimes we said yes. I can't say exactly what we were doing or why we had to do it. During the day, we were in charge of classes that ran from 9-4 and were so intensive our students sometimes broke down and cried. Later at night while lesson planning, many of us cried, too. Some of us were teaching excerpts of Foucault's *Discipline and Punish: The Birth of the Prison* and we were thinking about how "docile bodies" functioned in institutional landscapes like prisons, hospitals, and schools.

There are odd moments when you teach students texts that if they truly believed and took to heart, would cause them to throw up their desks in protest and walk out. They almost never do, and so you fantasize about what it would mean to live out these ideas on your own. You dance to free your docile body from the work of the institution that never pays enough and makes all of the rules. You dance to become a mute animal, who has no responsibilities and her own kind of power.

Dancing can lead to fucking, but it mostly it's about joy and possibility. Its energy comes from potential community, loose collectives, affinities, and affiliations. Dancing can reclaim a space and give it a make-over. It refutes the docile body, reclaims it, and animates it from within. The liberation is brief, but necessary. *Your body is your own! Even just for this one song!* It's the heart that responds most enthusiastically to the beat of a song, and in institutions, it's often the heart that needs resuscitation.

I taught for many summers in this program. Each summer the teachers had a favorite song. The best was OutKast's "Hey Ya," which was so powerful that whenever anyone put it on, no matter what state we were in—drunk and passed out, lesson planning, napping, showering, or walking to the dining hall—we'd all come running and dance or fake dance depending on how exhausted or ironic we felt. The song kept us moving, even if the dancing was robotic and phoned-in, though mostly because of Andre 3000's enthusiasm, it wasn't.

Girlfriend Is Better

In my course, *Youth in Revolt*, we pay close attention to what often gets called passive or soft resistance—subversive fashion, music, zine making, flash mobs and dancing. According to Jon Savage in his book *Teenage: the Creation of Youth Culture,* during World War II, swing dancing teens in Germany and Paris turned "adolescent obnoxiousness into street theater, they offered a symbolic resistance to the occupation's 'ambient, abstract horror,' that also mirrored its ultimate vacancy" (390). Dance, and particularly swing with its appropriation of black American style and rhythm was an offense punishable by hanging in the Nazi party, who demanded total body and mind control of its youth.

At the marches I attend to protest Trump, I find myself thinking of Savage's language.

Street theater.

Ambient, abstract horror.

Ultimate vacancy.

Early in Trump's presidency, I marched with hundreds of protesters to Goldman Sachs to resist his appointment of Steve Mnuchin as Secretary of Treasury. I chanted next to a drummer, who painted "End the Ban" on his drum. The drum kept me moving. None of us danced, but I appreciated the beat, our hand-made signs, and a return to some anti-banking chants I haven't heard since Occupy Wall Street. As we marched past the Goldman Sachs building, located on its own side street with a beautiful, glittery canopy, I stared into the lobby. Empty except for security guards in their oversized suits. I thought of the sub-prime housing crisis—and how so many banks and bankers profited from what was to them a purely abstract horror. I remembered how much I hate suits—wearing them, seeing others wearing them, and how I just couldn't get behind the whole Hillary pantsuit craze.

I remembered my father gleefully playing me The Talking Head's song "Girl Friend is Better" in our upstate New York living room in the eighties. In the video, David Byrne dons his now famous giant suit and croons about who took the money away. I think of my father, whom I barely speak to anymore, who was an accountant and wore a suit every day for all his adult working life. He wanted to be a writer. When he came home from the office, he shrugged off his suit and lounged around the house in his underwear while my mother and us kids brought him dinner, the paper, and beers.

That suit paid for a lot.

That suit cost us a lot, too.

It's an act of resistance to refuse to refuse suits and make art in a country that tells you every day that you are worth very little.

My student, Felipe, taught me to consider the power of the suit, how it can equalize power and allow for access and mobility.

But it has to be a really good suit, I think.

And what if you subvert the suit? Make it big and weird? Or tight and inappropriate? What if you dance in it and make it a puppet for your body?

Excursions

Around the same time my father was forcing me to listen to the Talking Heads, I was sneaking out of the house to go to gay bars. I met my first drag queen at one of the two gay bars in my hometown when I was sixteen. I snuck in. I had never in my life seen anyone so commanding and beautiful. Afterwards, she gave me an autograph. The place was called the Nite Spot. It was 1987. I had one or two friends who were out of the closet with their closest friends but not to the general population of our homophobic high school or their parents. I must have gone with one of them.

As an undergraduate, still in upstate New York, but in a bigger, more cosmopolitan college town, I danced only at gay bars and house parties. One night, at someone's sprawling five-bedroom house, A Tribe Called Quest's *Low End Theory*, we listened to the whole album, twice through.

I hated the straight bars, which were full of sorority sisters and fraternity brothers and smelled like vomit after a certain hour. I'd had my fill of the jocks, cheerleaders, and rednecks with baseball bats in pick-up trucks who chased us around, hoping to corner us on some empty street. It wasn't all that different from Richard Linklater's movie *Dazed and Confused,* only less fun. Besides, the music at gay bars was always better and many of my closest friends were gay men and women.

Risky Business.

Sometimes we drove to Ithaca to go to *The Haunt.*

My friend Ed's high kicks to songs that he really really loved. Usually Stevie Nicks.

Club 81.

The back room of Club 81 sold merchandise that I coveted but never had enough money to buy. There was a watch that looked like a collar that the bartender sometimes let me try on.

A man alone in the middle of the dance floor, dancing slowly and totally to his own beat while we all watched.

The back alley behind *Club 81,* where we smoked and talked and exchanged numbers. I made out with someone back there. A couple of times.

The dance floor had a disco ball and a mirrored wall. Watching yourself. Watching everyone else.

I learned a lot about hooking up in these bars. Have I always had a gay man inside of me or as my wingman who loves to cruise or did I just learn how to flirt from gay men?

I look at you. "You're cute," I shout drunkenly in your ear. I call you over.
I yell at you. Sometimes you ignore me, but mostly it works. I kiss you.
I remember one of my college boyfriends saying to me that I should distance myself from my gay friends because hanging out with them made me undesirable to straight men.

How many men have said to me *Slow down, Take it easy, Hang back, Let me make the first move?* In my 20s, I was often accused of being too aggressive, too forward, and too determined. How relieved I am that I no longer listen to these men.

I learned how to dance alone and in solidarity on those dance floors. I learned how to speak up and say what I wanted. Queer dance floors taught me that the straight male gaze didn't have to matter so much. I needed that. We all do.

New Boys

On June 11, 2016, Omar Mateen, a 29-year old security guard, killed 49 people and wounded 53 others in a terrorist attack inside the Pulse night club in Orlando during Latin night. It was the largest terrorist attack against the LGBTQ community in U.S. history. Like many New Yorkers, I attended a vigil outside of the now historic Stonewall Inn, and for most of the week, I walked by Stonewall and stood in the pocket park in front of it where people had left candles and signs for the victims. I didn't do much there. I read the signs and I thought about my friends. I lingered for too long and made myself late for the class I was teaching.

I read a lot of poems and essays that week. Every time I read, Christopher Soto's "All the Dead Boys Look Like Me" I cried. The same thing happened when I read Roy G. Guzmán's "Restored Mural for Orlando." Soto and Guzman reminded me of the parts of my ethnicity I don't know very well. I remembered the story of my Cuban grandma's little brother who died in New York of a heart attack on the very same day as his own father. He had a long-term girlfriend, but my grandpa insisted he was gay and made mariposa jokes about him even after he was dead. I thought of all the students in my 20 years of teaching who have come out to me in their writing and in office hours and about the ways I have tried to flip my classroom—to make it the queerest, most female, most of color space I can because that's how the world feels to me. Rooms full of straight white people make me nervous and queasy.

What does it mean to be a quarter Cuban? How do I situate that next to my three quarters of Swedish, German, English, and Spanish which allow me to reap the fucked-up privileges that go hand in hand with my sun-burning skin? Is this ethnic fractioning like my sexuality which is mostly one thing and a little bit another? What do I mean when I tell my father that I'm mostly straight but have a queer sensibility?

It means I feel "mixed" about a lot of shit. If you give me a problem, I will feel two to ten ways about it. I speak from multiple positions. Sometimes I need to shut up and listen and sometimes I need to speak up. I pass for one thing, but sometimes feel like another. I feel like an ally and a spy.

The essay is my most comfortable genre because it allows me to honestly change my mind. I like landscapes that feel like mixed tapes and I'll take a queer dance floor over a straight one.

When I read Justin Torres' "In Praise of Latin Night at the Queer Club," I got angry and then defiant. Maybe I was channeling that first drag queen I met, who came to my backwards upstate town to do whatever the hell she wanted. It was her show. We could watch it or not. Or maybe I was feeling the power of Torres' writing:

> Outside, tomorrow, hangovers, regrets, the grind. Outside, tomorrow, the struggle to effect change. But inside, tonight, none of that matters. Inside, tonight, the only imperative is to love. Lap the bar, out for a smoke, back inside, the ammonia and sweat and the floor slightly tacky, another drink, the imperative is to get loose, get down, find religion, lose it, find your hips locked into another's, break, dance on your own for a while — but you didn't come here to be a nun — find your lips pressed against another's,

break, find your friends, dance. The only imperative is to be transformed, transfigured in the disco light. To lighten, loosen, see yourself reflected in the beauty of others. You didn't come here to be a martyr, you came to live, papi. To live, mamacita. To live, hijos. To live, mariposas.

I keep thinking about the outside/inside binary that Torres lays out for us, and there are other binaries lurking underneath the surface of that one—work/play, activism/fun, and day/night. For Torres, the dance floor's imperative, especially the queer Latinx one—is to be transformed and transfigured, and to see yourself in the beauty of someone else. You're not a martyr. You're a dancer and you deserve to live.

These small acts matter even more in a time of state-sanctioned hate. Claim your space. Dance in defiance. Fuck who you want and on your own terms. Love is your only imperative.

Right before the Pulse shooting, a student gave me a song by Lust for Youth, a Swedish pop confection that sounds exactly like New Order.

So are you ready
Let it burn through colours
Feels like you're falling
but it passes in time
into a better day
Feels like you're falling
but it passes in your mind
into a better day
Feels like you're falling
but it passes in time
into a better day
our hearts
our heads

I've never heard it in a club and I've only danced to it my living room. It became my mourning song. Falling. Passing. In time. A better day.

Certain dance floors offer a nameless kind of oblivion—an oceanic feeling where you can lose yourself to the mass of bodies or become one with another, sometimes faceless, body. In her essay "Joy," Zadie Smith explores the difference between pleasure and joy and argues that "joy is such a human madness" and that pleasure is easier to name than joy (151). Of her pleasures, she lists, "an egg sandwich from one of the grimy food vans on Washington Square," a "pineapple popsicle" and staring at "other people's faces" (145-146). Joy, for Smith, is a "strange mixture of terror, pain, and delight" (147). In my favorite part of the essay, she recounts a joy-filled night on Ecstasy in 1999 in London at a place called the Fabric Club. She remembers:

> All was dance floor. Everybody danced. I stood still, oppressed on all sides by dancing, quite sure I was about to go out of my mind. Then suddenly I could hear Q-Tip—blessed Q-Tip!—not a synthesizer, not a vocoder, but Q-Tip, with his human voice, rapping over a human beat.
>
> And the top of my skull opened to let human Q-Tip in, and a rail thin man with enormous eyes reached across a sea of bodies for my hand...I took the man's hand. The top of my head flew away. We danced and danced. We gave ourselves to joy. (148)

Smith understands that joy can be drug-induced and D.J.-fueled, but in our most joyous states, sometimes with the help of Q-Tip, our brains let go and we just dance. I've never taken Ecstasy, but I've done my fair share of acid and blow, and while cocaine induces a kind of chatty pleasure, it's acid that has, at times, made the top of my head joyously fly off.

Before I took acid or was ever even drunk, I went to a concert featuring New Order, PIL and The Sugar Cubes in Darien Lake, NY, in 1988, with three of my best friends. After we had our minds blown by the sight of Bjork wailing at us from atop twenty feet high speaker stacks and Johnny Lydon spit on us from the stage, we surged forward when New Order came out just after dusk. The sky was a dome of stars above the amphitheater's half shell. Steady drum machine beat. One body jumping. Hot press. Hands on my back and shoulders. We pogoed until my best friend fainted and we revived her by pouring sugar packets into her mouth, and then we started dancing again.

Later, in 1991, I visited a guy I'd met at a party upstate, a philosophy graduate student at the New School who lived on St. Marks near the mouth of Tompkins Square Park. We went to a Butthole Surfers concert. It was my first weekend in New York City. I was high on walking around, thumbing through records in tiny shops, and sitting on the dirty grass in Washington Square Park. When Gibby Haynes took the stage, the graduate student handed me his leather biker's jacket and waded out into the mosh pit. I looked on with the resigned jealously I always felt about mosh pits. I wanted to lose myself in there, but I was small and I didn't want to get punched, and so I held his coat, like so many punk girls in the late 80s and early 90s. We were waiting for the Riot Girls to invite us to the front, but we didn't know it yet.

After my marriage ended, I went to a particular bar because usually around midnight, a man touched my hips and moved me closer to him. Later, another man did, and then another. That was how we danced there. Ass to cock. Grinding. I was lost then and I needed someone to take the lead. At that same bar, another man whispered in my ear just as I backed into him, *I thought you were gay.* I didn't answer or I shrugged. I met a woman there who stopped talking to me because she saw me speaking to another woman in the bathroom line. *I see how you are,* she texted me later from her car.

Don't Tell 'Em

In her beautiful essay and eulogy to a Chicago DJ named Timbuck2 in *Catapult,* "Nights a DJ Changed My Life," Stacie Williams remembers nights waiting in line to get into clubs and the dancing that made the work week bearable. She asks, "What did I learn about being a woman, about freedom and consent, about danger and fear, about independence or feminism, about sex and sexuality, while the bass was pumping and the lights were low? The DJ provides a soundtrack to a very specific type of education." For Williams it's a communion with friends and music—what she calls "the peak of Chicago blackness," but it's also about the ways in which men and women come together and apart on dance floors, the excitement and danger of it. Chemistry and connection. In the final section of the essay, Williams admits:

> There are no more clubs. There are late nights and early mornings but instead of alcohol or boys or music, there are diapers and spelling tests and little people yelling about what they do or do not want to eat while I try to steal some time to complete a mundane task, like washing my hair. My cleavage, which I used to proudly display like semi-precious jewels, disappeared when my breasts turned into food production facilities. It is not bad. Just very different. I've spun into a new, 33 RPM version of myself.

Though I know she'll be just fine in this newest version of herself, there's a part of me that wants to say, *Don't forget to dance! Moms need to dance!* We need to be reminded that our bodies belong to us and are not just for labor and care taking.

Williams' essay got me wondering about my own dance floor education. I'm not a natural dancer. I don't have a special grace or rhythm, but my body knows what to do with itself despite of my rare neurological disorder that kept me immobile and decidedly not dancing until I was twelve. I can't salsa or tango or do choreographed dance moves. I am not traditionally coordinated. My dancing feels punk and bouncy to me. I dance with abandon and I don't much care about style. I get into it, which is really the best thing we can do when we're doing pretty much anything. Commit to the shit.

My ass can do things while dancing and fucking that even I don't understand. What to say to the men who have told me that they know I'm part Cuban because of my ass? *Yeah, I've heard that before.*

Statement of fact. My ass is my grandma's. I have her body more than my mother's. Tits. Ass. Stomach. Curvy, with small ankles and a long neck.

Sometimes my kid grabs onto my hips and shakes them. "Your butt is sooooo jiggly," she says, and I laugh because I know she means it as a compliment.

It's taken me a long time to love my ass, but early on dancing and fucking became sites for self-love, and for doing things with my body that I couldn't anywhere else. I've always been rewarded for being smart and won people over with clever taunts and witty puns. I have been a failure at most sports. Yoga, dancing, and the elliptical machine work for me because they come with music.

Dance floors have taught me to explore the tension between commitment and abandon and how to be a joyous animal in the midst of a world that asks us to think too much. My body knows things my brain can never access. My brain is never as free as my body, but when I write essays, my brain comes close to dancing. I leap more in writing than I ever do on the ground, and I'm happy for any air I can get.

Epilogue

Seth and I keep going back to Bedlam. One time on a Friday, the bar was empty, but the D.J. kept spinning. I managed to attract the attention of the one straight man in the bar. He told me he was a Russian physicist and he kept buying me shots of whiskey. I didn't believe him. I kissed him a couple of times but kept myself firmly anchored to Seth. When he pushed me to go home with him, I said something I've been saying for years, "I can't. I'm with my friends."

After the New York City women's march. A Saturday. No banker bros. No marketing betches. There was woman who gave no fucks and who ruled the dance floor with high kicks and ass shaking. When Nicki Minaj came on, she and Seth bonded for a drunken rap duet dance off. The shots we did. The shots we talked about. The bartender charged us $13. The DJ hugged us good-bye. Seth and I smoked too many Parliaments and ate a torta on the corner of Avenue A and First Street at 4 am while we trash talked the Pesident.

You may have the White House and a lot of super ugly buildings, but we have the streets and the bars and the backrooms and the dance floors. We have the best sex and the coolest outfits and the most fun and we are all the colors and all the genders and, eventually, we're going to win.

LOST IN THE WOODS

Galactic Rabbits

Last May, I clicked on Galactic Rabbit's, aka Gala Mukomolova horo-scopes. I readied myself. I was in a fragile state, and Gala, who is my friend, writes such insightful horoscopes I sometimes cry after reading them. The night before I drank too much whiskey and tried to dance the semester away at an East Village bar. The after effects of my debauchery were intense. I hadn't managed to leave my apartment and it was late into the afternoon. My head throbbed and I decided in a hung over, self-pitying way that while I was capable of intense out-burst of fun and wildness, I was forever to be punished with solitude and deep bouts of loneliness.

I read Gala's opening letter to readers which included the heart-busting sentence, "There are those of us who have always felt alone in the world, intrepid, aliens in every community we find our-selves in," and then scrolled down to the entry for Gemini. In it, Gala writes about a rare phone call from her brother, his offer to help her if she needs money, and the relief of this gesture:

> Because it's embarrassing, I'll admit that I treasured those stories we read as children, the ones where the girl and her brother go off bravely into the woods and find a way to survive. They aren't brave at first, just lost. And yes the girl is clever. She feeds the wild cat and knows what lights the dark heart of the forest witch. But her brother is her champion. Not because he is bigger or stronger—and he might be—but because he sees in her a great power and vows to protect it. In my heart, my brother and I are those children.

Isn't this what all lost children do? Find a way to survive. Partner up. Hunker down. Escape. Gala's story about her brother spoke to me because, like many children who emerged from less than ideal childhoods, I have long thought of my brother as the Hansel to my Gretel. Somehow long ago, we'd made a pact in the woods to protect each other. It was a fairy tale we told ourselves.

My brother recently sent me a text that he had the potential in his new business to do well and that if that happened, he would take care of me. I didn't press it. We text occasionally and talk on the phone hardly ever. When we see each other, I feel close to him, but we have long chunks of time when we don't communicate at all. Part of me didn't believe him, and part of me felt stunned by the love of it. And yet I've learned to expect no help from anyone, and to believe only in myself. *Why is my brother still offering to take care of me? Does my life look that precarious? Is this what adult children do? Is there something inherently worrisome about me as a single, divorced, American mom?* I wondered.

Maybe I didn't believe him because I've lost the ability to believe that anyone I know in this country can succeed in that wild, hopeful, American Dream, middle-class way. If 47% of Americans (and I'm one of them) would have a hard time coming up with $400 in an emergency, and our government continues to care so little for this reality, how could I believe in a windfall, family or otherwise (Gabler)? And yet like many Americans, I suspect I am tethered to two conflicting ideas. Sometimes I think if I scrimp and save enough I just might make it and to the whole bootstraps bullshit of the American dream way. Other times, I wallow in my own financial failures. Why do I still live paycheck to paycheck? What is wrong with me that I have so much debt?

And I'm honestly confused about how families help each other. Aside from splitting the cost of my undergraduate state school education in the early nineties, my parents have never given me any money. I have friends who have used family money for apartment down payments or college tuition for their children or who are expecting inheritances when their parents pass away. I have other friends like me who go it alone. I know people who are broke but if they had any extra money would give it to their kids or friends in a heartbeat. I went on a bad date with a man who'd been unemployed for five years, living with his sister and paying no rent. When I asked him if he ever felt like he should contribute, he waved me off, "It's family. This is what we do." I ran away so fast from that date that I fell into a snowbank. I couldn't see his arrangement with his sister as anything other than a grift. I feared he was just looking for another woman to feed and house him. Still, I understand that in the absence of any substantial government intervention--a living minimum wage, national subsidized child care, and a real commitment to affordable housing—our nebulous and complicated relationships with family members are what's left.

As I write this essay, I scroll through my friends' Instagram feeds. It's Pride in NYC, and I am filled as usual with a weeping love for the queer friends that have held me, loved me, and become my family. I take in the shirtless photos and signs that read "Gays Against Guns: GAG!" and "Yo Soy Pulse!" From my window I hear the roars of joy from the parade. I have a stupid, stubborn hope that love will win and that the world is changing for the better, that we are in the last ugly, violent, bloody throes of rape culture, patriarchy, and a racist system that is dying, but so slowly that it almost doesn't feel like a death at all.

All is not lost, I keep telling myself. *There are new maps and new families and those who are lost will find a way to catch up.*

Lost Boy

Once my brother and I actually got lost in the woods. We were at Alleghany State Park for my father's annual office picnic (an event I would later appreciate for its drunken contours) but at the time it just seemed like a really good party for kids. Unlimited cans of grape soda! Pringles poured out of the canister into giant bowls! *Let's dig a hole to China on the beach!* One year my father puked into our plastic beach bucket as my mother drove the car home with us in the front seat with her. Another year, my mother cried on the sidewalk outside of our house, and my father had to beg her to come inside.

There was a path into the woods from the picnic site. We took it. There were other kids, too. Chatter. Bravado. A girl my age named Beth whose father owned a boat. She had a beautiful Dorothy Hamill haircut that worked because her hair was thick not fine like mine and a new young stepmom who wore high-heeled sandals. Her little sister Amy was cute and petulant. I wanted to impress them and got caught up in the stories we each told about the stupidity of sixth grade. "Some girls are wearing make-up while others are playing with Cabbage Patch dolls!" we might have exclaimed at each other.

It was late in the day, and I was walking, so this was post-recovery after a doctor in Toronto gave me a magical pill that changed my life and made it possible for me to walk again. Maybe I was high on that freedom. I could walk anywhere! Maybe I remembered the little patch of woods between houses in our old neighborhood where a boy who was two years older and I stripped naked and pressed our bodies together. Front side. Back side. Electricity. Maybe I understood at that early moment in the woods with that boy that I was a witch or that I'd pretty much do anything for sex because it meant pleasure and escape. Probably not. Everything I did then was underground, unconscious, and subterranean. Motives were not something I could identify accurately in myself until my late thirties.

"My dad will be mad," Beth said, speaking the universal eighties code for spanking and grounding. They wanted to go back, so we waved good-bye to their haltered, sunburned shoulder blades and kept walking. Maybe we were running away. Maybe we were on an adventure. Maybe my brother was excited that I could finally walk somewhere with him. He'd been playing in the woods next to a new housing development up the road from our house for the last year and coming home with small snakes, which he kept in shoeboxes with holes in them until they escaped. Maybe we'd already seen *E. T.* and *Goonies* and we believed in the power of children to change the narrative of adult lives. Our parents didn't seem to like each other very much. Maybe we wanted to walk away from that sad reality. Maybe we were just having fun.

Somehow, we got turned around. We wound up on a different path by trees we didn't recognize. The woods got thicker and the path more narrow. Eventually, the path opened up onto what we thought was the office picnic, but instead was an empty ranger's station and a road with no cars on it. The scene was eerily quiet, like a set from *The Twilight Zone*. There's was no park ranger or any other hikers and definitely no other kids. The sun was starting to set. We chose another path, and then another, but they all looked unfamiliar and wrong. We were not calm kids. My brother regularly entertained fears of getting kidnapped by a man in a non-descript white van. I had never recovered from watching *Poltergeist* and believed at any moment that a tree could swallow me whole.

We followed one of the paths back towards the abandoned Ranger station. We looked closely at the map pinned to the wall, but we couldn't read it. We didn't know where we'd been, and the map didn't look anything like the ones my parents kept crumple-folded under the passenger seat of our Toyota Corolla. It had blue lines on it to indicate topography, but no "x" to indicate where we stood.

"We have to just walk," I said.

"But which way?" my brother looked more panicked than I'd ever seen him.

"If we just get on a path and stick with it, we'll find them," I lied and started to lead us down the path that felt right to me.

My brother fell behind me on the path, silently crying. It was almost dark. "We can't be alone in the woods at night," he sobbed.

"Don't cry," I maybe said.

He rushed forward and hugged me, clung to me really, and stammered, "You have to help us. You have to figure it out. You're the oldest. It's your job."

I hugged him back and patted his back. I realized for all of his farting bravado in our family room, his figure-four leg locks, and his ability to dribble around all of the soccer players in his league, he was still only nine. Something in me clicked into place, and I knew that no matter how afraid I was, I had to hide it from him and get us back to the picnic. I was the oldest. He was too scared to think straight. I had to find our way.

Somehow, I picked the right path. It's possible that all the paths led to the picnic area and we just needed to commit to one, and I'd helped us do that. I started to recognize certain trees. I kept us moving, and I refused to cry.

It was dark when we got back to the picnic site and all the parents were packing up. It never occurred to us that any of them would come looking for us, and they didn't.

"Beth said you were just behind her," my mother said as she folded our lawn chairs into the hatchback. "So, we've just been waiting."

We drove home in silence. Our parents were mad, but they couldn't grasp or we couldn't speak to the enormity of what we'd just experienced. We were lost in the woods. We thought it was forever, but we found our way back. We were Hansel and Gretel without the breadcrumbs. What scared me most of all was that our parents didn't even really get it. I saw then that they couldn't protect us forever and that we were capable of getting hopelessly lost while they were distracted or fighting or having fun.

I am your little mother. Take my hand, and I'll show you the way. I'm clever. I know the witch. I am the moon. I can churn butter and sew a dress. I'm plump and dimpled, though there are hard lines across my body. Let's call them Chin, Nose, and Face. Don't cross them. I am the map. The topography's inside of me. Let's call it blood. I am the lost twin. I'm Gemini and I'm always looking for you and you and you and you. I was made for pleasure. I was made for work. I can find a needle in a haystack and any boy, in any woods, any where. Except for that one little boy, who got away.

Re-Birth

My pregnancy began as a twin pregnancy. We lost the other baby at the end of the fourth month. We'd already named him and the loss terrified and saddened me in a way I'd never experienced before. Still, I didn't allow myself to grieve. No one knew why that baby died, and the rest of the pregnancy was high risk. I felt I needed to focus on the other baby and do everything I could to get her out of me alive.

Recently, because she is seven now and we were talking about how she was born, I decided to tell my daughter about her twin. I wanted her to know, but I didn't want to tell her too soon. I explained it in as matter of fact way as I could. *You were once a twin. There was another baby, but he died before you were born.*

In the way that all major parenting events don't happen the way you thought they would or can't be planned, my daughter's responses surprised me.

First, she asked, "Why didn't you tell me sooner?" which was a perfectly good question.

"I wanted you to be old enough to understand," I managed, and then realized and added, "And also I was sad for a long time about it and it took me a while."

Then, maybe because she is a Leo, she said, "It's okay Mama, I like being an only child."

"Yeah, it's pretty nice, isn't it?" I said. It was a Saturday morning. We were cuddling in bed.

"What was his name?"

"Sal."

"What kind of name is that?"

"It's from a book Daddy loved and also that was his grandfather's name."

"You like old names."

"Yeah, we do."

And then she suggested we pretend she was being born again and I went with it because what else was going on that Saturday morning? She play acted a baby's high pitched cries and I pretended to push her out again under the quilt and it was silly and healing in a way I couldn't have ever imagined.

Since then, she has told close friends about her lost twin. These sweet girls have listened intently and one even added a story about the baby her mother lost before she was born. In my daughter's later re-enactments, her twin was born with her and then died. She treats this story as her own, mutable and changing depending on each performance. I have not corrected the details. We can return to those later. It's her story. Perhaps not even mine to write about. That was her twin, her brother, her lost boy. Gone long ago into the cosmos, where desire and longing and mourning swirl around in a galactic stew. If this galaxy could speak to us, it might say, *Where are you going? Who are you looking for? What have you lost?*

Recently, while walking in a cemetery with her dad, she asked, "Do you think he's here?" Around that same time, she told us that she doesn't like it when people say she's lucky to be an only child. "Because I might have wanted a brother," she said to us as she bounced on top of one the couch cushions.

I suspect that her feelings about her lost twin will change and change again. I can't know what it's like for her to have been a twin and to have lost a future brother before he was born. Did she feel him swimming next to her? Were they communicating inside the womb? Did she know when his heart stopped beating? These are cosmic questions. Hard to ask and unanswerable.

I suppose, in talking to her and in writing about it, I've accepted that loss, grieved for that baby that never quite was, and still he was a little boy who got away, the one I couldn't save. I was not to be his little mother. Nor she.

Star Light

When I was seventeen, I visited a psychic in the small town of Lily Dale, New York, the spiritualist capital of the world and just a half hour away from my hometown. I went to the same psychic my father saw once a year. I'm not sure why he went—he's a hardcore atheist and scoffs at most anything that's not science-based, but he liked her and said she was the real-deal. I believe her name was Anna May Dodd, though my Googling can't confirm this, and she's long since passed away. As Goth/punk teenagers, my friends and I were drawn to Lily Dale, though we often did no more than wander the grounds and marvel at the small tombstones in the pet cemetery.

She met me on her porch, and we stayed there for the duration of the reading. She told me nothing about my future, but she described my life to me in a way that felt miraculous. She understood the dynamics of my falling-apart family and she told me that I would make it out. She described my parents and their complicated, toxic dynamic, and when she got to my brother, she paused to wave to a neighbor on the barely paved street, and then continued.

"You can't forget about him when you go. He needs you. You have to take care of him."

I nodded, struck by the urgency of her tone.

"Is something going to happen?" I asked.

She shook her head no. "I have a brother, too," she offered and moved onto something else. I left her porch that day stunned and grateful because I felt profoundly seen, visible somehow in this seventy-year-old woman's light. I felt similarly when I met my current therapist four years ago. Somehow this person knew even though we'd never met.

Was that psychic right? Did my brother need my protection? Who was watching out for me? I still feel that I failed my brother because I left our small, shitty town and went to college in the midst of my parents' messy and bitter divorce. Three years later, he left for school, too. Perhaps I've cast a psychic net of care and love around him. I hope so, but I really can't say for sure. We're adults now. We have a close but careful relationship. There's so much I want to say to him, but I'm not brave enough yet to do it.

Still, I no longer feel like we're living in the woods. We're not those lost children anymore. In fact, when I text him about his memory of that day, he doesn't remember any of the details. *Was it an office picnic? Were there other kids involved?* he texts me back, and I'm left to wonder why my own memory is so intense and cinematic. Is it because I write? Does my brain excel at turning images into stories? My brother is often the only fact checker I have, and unlike me, he lives very much in the present.

I am not your little mother, though I can be very tender. If she calls me Mama, I do what she wants. I'm weak that way. I'm drawn to lost boys and Peter Pans.

You don't need a map anymore. You know the way. The path is lit up. There are fireflies or small lanterns. X marks the spot. Keep walking. Keep moving. Look up at the stars. The galaxy sees you. Ask your questions. Wait for answers in the stars.

SMALL ANIMAL, BIG ANIMAL

1

One of my favorite cartoon characters as a little girl was *Chilly Willy* the penguin. In my memory of Chilly Willy, Chilly and his polar bear friend Maxie battle the elements of Alaska and search for food. Sometimes Maxie is so hungry that he fantasizes that Chilly is a sausage. He chases him! Chilly runs! A lot! Until Chilly finds a stash of whole fish (protein!) and begins to throw fish into Maxie's mouth. I found Chilly's mute cuteness appealing as a child. My father had many nicknames for me and one of them was Chilly Willy. I have a high voice that often reminds people of cartoon characters or Jennifer Tilly. In my twenties, a string of guys I knew had on-going fantasies that I would be become a voice-over actor and have my own cartoon character. One guy I briefly dated, who worked freelance for Nickelodeon and kept a folder in his living room titled, "Got Stoned, Had an Idea," went so far as to create this character for me. Her name was Amber Ant and she had a lot to say and way too much on her plate.

When I Googled *Chilly Willy* episodes, I didn't find much except a Wikipedia entry and some You Tube videos. I watched some of the videos and saw that I was all wrong about Chilly. It's Chilly who is always hungry and cold, not Maxie. In one episode, he fantasizes about a winter coat and goes to the winter coat outlet to try to steal one. In another called "Half-Baked Alaska" Chilly shivers in the snow and sees a sign for a restaurant. When he arrives, Smedley the dog, his foil, is running the restaurant. Smedley thinks he's found a paying customer and brings Chilly a stack of pancakes slathered in butter and syrup.

"More syrup? More jelly? More whipped cream?" Smedley asks as Chilly nods repeatedly.

But as soon as Chilly is about to take a bite, Smedley pulls away the plate, unfurls a bill for sixty dollars, and says, "Pay first, eat later."

Chilly's disappointment is palpable. He sheds a tear and pulls at his empty pockets. For the rest of the episode, Chilly tries to work as a piano player, a barber, a blacksmith's assistant, and a photographer's assistant to pay for the pancakes. Eventually, Chilly steals pancakes from Smedley, but then rescues Smedley from an irate customer. Smedley calls him a "customer for life" and serves him a stack of pancakes. Chilly may not be able to hold down a job, but he's good at finding a big animal to take care of him.

Created by Walter Lantz, the genius behind Woody Woodpecker, Chilly operates in a landscape of Depression era food longing and kid gluttony. What if you could eat all the pancakes? What if you were never hungry or cold? What if your parental figure/giant polar bear friend was able to hunt enough fish for you to eat?

I have always known that cartoon characters were early erotic fantasies for me, and I've written about this before in a poem about Mighty Mouse. But Lantz, like many animators at the time, was particularly good at turning me on. I still get a little wet when I think about an episode of Woody Woodpecker when he dressed in drag to lure a stagecoach driver into picking him up. He used a decoy leg— one in fishnet stockings and a high heel—to signal the stagecoach driver. This leg served as early masturbation fodder.

I have always been interested in the idea of a small animal that cares for a larger one. The first short story I ever wrote in fourth grade was about a clown shrimp—a small parasite that lives off the dead skin of a fish. No one suggested to me that this was weird. Wait, is it? I have long loved the story of the mouse who picks the thorn out of the lion's paw. I find all these stories vaguely erotic. Tiny and big, working together. Tiny does something for big and is rewarded with protection. Big does not eat Tiny. Tiny has all the power, actually, but will occasionally pretend she does not and run around pretending to be scared. Tiny feeds big, but is actually quite a little glutton herself. I suppose in BDSM circles, we might call this topping from the bottom or being a switch.

It's possible, too, that my father saw me as Chilly and he was my polar bear. One of the many jobs my brother and I had to do for our father was to bring him food and beers. Like many children of that era, we were also expected to stand in front of the television and change the channel until my father found what he wanted to watch. After he settled on a football game or a Godzilla movie, he said, "Go fix me a sandwich," to whichever one of us hadn't scurried quickly back to the couch to nest in the crook of his arm.

Like the good waiter child I'd been trained to be, I'd dutifully respond, while giving my brother the stink eye, "Do you want mayo or mustard or both? Salami or ham?"

"Salami. Did your mother buy any cheese?"

"I think we ran out," I might have said.

"Put pepperoncinis on it?" my father sighed. "Are there chips?"

"We ate them all."

"Then just bring me a beer with the sandwich."

I did and then I settled into the other crook of my father's armpit to watch whatever he was watching.

2

When I first started dating a couple of years ago after my marriage ended, I listed on my on-line dating profile that I was only interested in tall men. I wanted, like many women, to feel tiny, perhaps even more so because I'm not particularly small. I'm 5'5', which is above the average height for women and I weigh anywhere between 140 and 155 pounds. My first serious boyfriend after my marriage fit the bill. He was 6'3 and weighed 240 pounds. Sometimes after sex, I lay on top of his body, and felt like a small bird on top of a giant rock. Once when a drunk lurched towards me on the sidewalk, this same boyfriend imperceptibly put his body between mine and the staggering man's. Insta-shield! The man stopped short and veered off in the other direction towards his next victim. Other times, for fun, my giant boyfriend lay on top of me and pretended to crush me with his body. It was one of those games I've been playing with boys since before I can remember. *How much can you stand? Does this hurt? What about this?*

"Go ahead put your full weight on me," I said.

"That's not going to work. I'll crush you," he said.

"I can handle it."

"No, you can't."

"Yes, I can."

Shrug. "Okay."

And then he settled half of his full-weight on top of me. Leg to leg. Dick to pussy. Chest to chest. Face to face.

"See?" I said haughtily.

"You want more?" he raised his eyebrows at me.

"Yes."

"Okay," he lowered his chest more fully onto mine.

"It's too much," I screamed after about 15 seconds. "I can't breathe." He rolled off of me. Giggling. This was our foreplay.

Recently, I met a man who was exactly my height and who was so good in bed and so good at talking—jokes, questions, the news, food, stories, gossip—anything really, that I fell for him in one night. Swoop. Crash. My heart. But he was small. I weighed more than him. When my ex, the big boyfriend, asked me how I felt about this, I could only say, *I don't care*. Because suddenly I didn't anymore.

It didn't work out with this small man and I was sad for two months, but I learned that I can be a big animal and that sometimes I like it.

3

We watched *Finding Dory* in a newly re-furbished AMC in the East Village that has fully reclining seats, which are not unlike beds. Because *Finding Dory* is harrowing and involves a disabled fish who was separated from her parents as a child and is trying to find them once again as an adult, I couldn't fall asleep as I sometimes do in these weird movie seat beds. I loved *Finding Nemo* for its anti-helicopter parenting message and the weird fish who were trapped in dentist's office fish tank. My favorite was Gill, who proves to Nemo that he can take care of himself with a simple fish nod and a "You know what to do."

My daughter squirmed next to me on her bed seat as the drama unfolded. I cried in the opening scene and she looked over at me in mild disgust,

"Mama, you're crying already."

"Yeah, that's going to happen more," I said and grabbed for her hand.

She held it for a while and then let it go so she could dig deeply into her sack of sour patch kids.

I see now that *Finding Dory* is all about the big animal, small animal dynamic. Dory, Nemo, and Marlin rely on big animals—mostly an amazingly grouchy octopus—named Hank—to help them navigate the aquarium, find each other, and escape. In turn, the smaller animals teach the big animals to break free but stay together. Hank gives up his hermit dream of being alone and moving to an aquarium in Cleveland. Small animals get something physical they need, namely transport and protection, while the big animals get wisdom and insight.

I suppose I am my daughter's big animal, and this is a movie about alternative family structures. Birth families and adoptive families. Queer fish and disabled outsiders. Community. And not giving up and moving to Cleveland, no matter what.

When you give birth, the doctor puts this tiny screaming animal baby on you and you try to feed it, and it sort of works and it sort of doesn't and you keep going. You strap the baby to your body and you walk around and it takes a couple of years, but soon the baby is a kid and the kid is walking away from you. Coming back still, but also walking away. Trying out its small legs on this large, stupid, dangerous planet. Those small legs are ridiculous. How can that small person be walking while wearing skinny jeans no less? Why are they walking off a curb? Eventually that small person can talk about her feelings and is living with her dad half the time in Brooklyn and when she is with you, she treats your big animal body like a rock in the ocean. She washes up onto your shores. She scrambles somehow up the side of you. She hits you like a wave you'll never stop surfing.

4

I turned 44 on the summer solstice and strawberry moon. On my walk home from a dinner with one of my best friends, I felt a great release. For the last three and half years, I'd been walking around like a wound in search of a bandage or maybe just another wound. I thought it was my right to have a partner. I felt entitled to a spouse. As a small animal, I was supposed to be given a big animal. *Where did my big animal go? Why have all the big animals stopped taking care of me?*

As I stood in the mist of the Washington Square Park fountain, I realized I could play with big animals and small animals, but maybe I didn't need any animals to take care of me.

WORKS CITED

Amirpour, Ana Lily director. *A Girl Walks Home Alone at Night*. Kino Lorber, 2014.

Barthes, Roland. *Camera Lucida*. Hill and Wang, 1980.

Bazelon, Emily. "Why America Should Outlaw Spanking." *Slate*. 25 January, 2007.

Bechdel, Allison. *Are You My Mother?: a Comic Drama*. Mariner Books, 2013.

Bellamy, Dodie. "The Beating of Our Hearts." *When the Sick Rule the World*. Semiotext(e). 2015, 160-180.

Easton, Dosie and Hardy, Janet W. *The Ethical Slut: A Practical Guide to Polyamory, Open Relationships, and Other Adventures*. Greenery Press, 1997.

Ehrenriech, Barbara. *Bright-Sided: How Positive Thinking is Undermining America*. Picador. 2010.

Faber, Adele and Mazlish, Elaine. *How to Talk So Kids Will Listen and Listen So Kids Will Talk*. Scriber, 2012.

Fateman, Johanna. "Women on the Verge: On Art, Feminism, and Social Media." *Art Forum*. April 2015. www.artforum.com/inprint/issue=201504&id=50736

Fiennes, Sophie, director. *The Pervert's Guide to Ideology Featuring Slavoj Zizek*. Doc Club, 2012.

Frederickson, Caroline. "There is No Excuse for How Universities Treat Adjuncts." *Atlantic Monthly*. 15 September 2015. www.theatlantic.com/business/archive/2015/09/higher-education-college-adjunct-professor-salary/404461/

Gabler, Neal. "The Secret Shame of Middle Class Americas." *The Atlantic Monthly*. May 2016. www.theatlantic.com/magazine/archive/2016/05/my-secret-shame/476415/

George, Madeleine. *Seven Homeless Mammoths Wander New England*. Samuel French, 1999.

Gillepsie, Craig, director. *Lars and the Real Girl*. Metro-Goldwyn-Mayer, 2007.

Gottlieb, Michael, director. *Mannequin.* Gladden Entertainment, 1987.

Graunt, John. *Natural and Political Observations Made Upon the Bills of Mortality.* 1662.

Guzmán, Roy G. "Restored Mural for Orlando." http://www. roygguzman.com/restored-mural-for-orlando/

Halberstam, Jack. *The Queer Art of Failure.* Duke University Press, 2011.

Heller, Marielle, director. *Diary of a Teenage Girl.* Caviar Films, 2015.

Hinken, Melanie. "Why Many Retired Women Live in Poverty." *CNN Money.* 13 May, 2014. http://money.cnn.com/2014/05/13/ retirement/retirement-women/index.html

Hollywood vs. History. Wild. Interview with Cheryl Strayed. http:// www.historyvshollywood.com/reelfaces/wild/

Hughes, John, director. *Weird Science.* Universal Pictures, 1985.

Jamison, Leslie. *The Empathy Exams.* Graywolf Press, 2014.

Johnson, Sophie Lucido. "A More Perfect Love." *Catapult.* 19 February, 2016. www.catapult.co/stories/a-more-perfect-love

Jonze, Spike, director. *Her.* Annapurna Pictures, 2013.

Junod, Tom. "In Praise of the 42-Year-Old Woman." *Esquire. July, 2014.*

Lawson, Guy. "The Dukes of Oxy: How a Band of Teen Wrestlers Built a Smuggling Empire." *Rolling Stone.* 9 April, 2015. http:// www.rollingstone.com/culture/features/the-dukes-of-oxy-how-a-band-of-teen-wrestlers-built-a-smuggling-empire-20150409

Li, YiYun. "Dear Friend, From My Life I Write to You in Your Life." *The Best American Essays.* Editor, John Jeremiah Sullivan. Houghton Mifflin Harcourt, 2014. 109-121.

Marshall, Penny, director. *Awakenings.* Columbia Pictures, 1990.

Martin, Dawn Lundy. "The Long Road to Angela Davis's Library." *The New Yorker.* 26 December, 2014. http://www.newyorker. com/books/page-turner/long-road-angela-davis-library

Massey, Alana. "The Dickonomics of Tinder." *Medium.* 30 April, 2015. http://www.medium.com/matter/ the-dickonomics-of-tinder-b14956c0c2c7

Miller, Alice. *The Drama of the Gifted Child.* Basic Books, 1981.

Moore, Tracy. "Breaking: *Esquire* Declares 42-Year-Old Women Now Fuckable." *Jezebel.* 10 July, 2014. http://www.jezebel. com/breaking-esquire-declares-42-year-old-women-now-fuckab-1603138491

Mukomolova, Gala. *Galactic Rabbit.* May 2016. http://www.galacti-crabbit.com/2016/05/galactic-rabbit-may-2016/

Naanes, Marlene. "An Unusual Business, 'Nitpicking' as a Day Job." *A.M. New York.* 31 August, 2009, http://www.vosizneias.com/post/read/37575/2009/08/31/borough-park-ny-an-unusual-business-nitpicking-as-a-day-job/.

New York City Census Data 2010-2014. http://maps.nyc.gov/census/.

O'Connell, Meaghan. "The Patronizing Questions We Ask Women Who Write." *New York Magazine.* 17 March, 2017. http://www.thecut.com/2016/03/patronizing-questions-we-ask-women-who-write.html

O'Connor, Maureen. In "The Big Secret of Every Dating App: Tech Doesn't Matter. *New York Magazine.* 5 October, 2015. http://www.thecut.com/2015/10/big-secret-of-every-dating-app.html

O'Connor, Maureen. "The Voltron Theory of Casual Dating." *New York Magazine.* 13 February, 2015. http://www.thecut.com/2015/02/voltron-theory-of-casual-dating.html

Philyaw Dessha and Thomas, Michael D. *Co-Parenting 101: Helping Your Kids Thrive in Two Households After Divorce.* New Harbingers Publications, 2013.

Preciado, Paul B. *Testo Junkie.* Feminist Press, 2013.

"Put a Bird On It." *Portlandia,* created and performed by Fred Armisen and Carrie Brownstein, season 1, episode 1, 2011.

Rubin, Gretchen. *The Happiness Project.* Harper. 2009.

Sales, Nancy Jo. "Tinder and the Dawn of the 'Dating Apocalypse.'" *Vanity Fair.* 6 August, 2015. http://www.vanityfair.com/culture/2015/08/tinder-hook-up-culture-end-of-dating

Savage, Jon. "German Swing Kids and French Zazous." *Teenage: the Creation of Youth Culture*. Penguin Books, 2008.

Schumer, Charles. "Official Press Release." 7 March, 2012. http://www.legistorm.com/stormfeed/view_rss/388590/member/85.html

Scott, Ridley, director. *Alien*. Twentieth Century Fox, 1979.

Senior, Jennifer. *All Joy and No Fun: the Paradox of Modern Parenting*. Ecco, 2015.

Singal, Jesse. "Has Tinder Really Sparked a Dating Apocalypse?" *New York Magazine*. 12 August, 2015. http://www.nymag.com/scienceofus/2015/08/has-tinder-really-sparked-a-dating-apocalypse.html

Smith, Kiki. "Rapture." Sculpture. 2001.

Smith, Kiki. "Tale." Sculpture. 1992.

Smith, Zadie. "Joy." *The Best American Essays 2014*. Editor, John Jeremiah Sullivan. Houghton Mifflin Harcourt, 2014, 145-151.

Soto, Christopher. "All the Dead Boys Look Like Me." *Lit Hub*. 15 June, 2016. http://lithub.com/all-the-dead-boys-look-like-me/

Spechler, Diana. "Breaking Up with My Meds." *The New York Times*. 2015. http://www.opinionator.blogs.nytimes.com/tag/going-off/

Spielberg, Steven, director. *A.I. Artificial Intelligence*. Warner Brothers, 2001.

Sontag, Susan. *Regarding the Pain of Others*. Picador, 2004.

Stanton, Andrew and MacLane, Andrew, directors. *Finding Dory*. Pixar, 2016.

"Suicide, Facts at a Glance." *Center for Disease Control*. http://www.cdc.gov/violenceprevention/pdf/suicide-datasheet-a.pdf

"Top Ten Street Names for Valium." *Addiction Blog*. 4 May, 2011. http://www.prescription-drug.addictionblog.org/top-10-street-names-for-valium-diazepam/

Torres, Justin. "In Praise of Latin Night at the Queer Club." *The Washington Post*. 13 June, 2016. http://www.washingtonpost.com/opinions/in-praise-of-latin-night-at-the-queer-club/2016/06/13/e841867e-317b-11e6-95c0-2a6873031302_story.html?utm_term=.88569643d494

Traister, Rebecca. "The Single American Woman." *New York Magazine.* 21 February, 2016. http://www.thecut.com/2016/02/political-power-single-women-c-v-r.html

Ulinich, Anya. *Lena Finkle's Magic Barrel.* Penguin Books, 2014.

Vallee, Jean-Marc, director. *Wild.* Fox Searchlight, 2014

Wallace, Benjamin. "Autism Spectrum: Are You On It?" *New York Magazine.* 12 May, 2014. http://www.nymag.com/news/features/autism-spectrum-2012-11/

Weems, Carrie Mae. "Kitchen Table Series." Photographs. 1990.

Westhale, July. "Loneliness and the Strange Alone-Togetherness of the Internet Age." *The Establishment.* 23 December, 2015. http://www.theestablishment.co/loneliness-and-the-strange-alone-togetherness-of-the-internet-age-3494ecc532c3

"What to Expect When You're Expecting." http://www.whattoexpect.com/pregnancy/symptoms-and-solutions/mucous-plug.aspx

Williams, Stacie. "Nights a DJ Changed My Life." *Catapult.* 19 April, 2016. http://www.catapult.co/stories/nights-a-dj-changed-my-life

Willingham, Emily "Of Lice and Men: An Itchy History." *Scientific American.* 14 February, 2011. http://www.blogs.scientificamerican.com/guest-blog/of-lice-and-men-an-itchy-history/

Wilson, Ronaldo V. "Obliteration Excavations 1: 'Para' to 'Para.'" *Harriot Blog.* The Poetry Foundation. 12 January, 2015. http://www.poetryfoundation.org/harriet/2015/01/obliteration-excavations-1-para-to-para

Yuknavitch, Lidia. *The Small Backs of Children.* Harper Perrenial, 2015.

ACKNOWLEDGEMENTS

For Clonazapam, Lexapro, Midol, Sinemet, and Zoloft.

For my therapist, Josh Jonas.

For my neurologist, Dr. Rachel Saunders-Pullman.

For Stephanie K. Hopkins, Matt Longabucco, and Jason Nunes, who read and gave me feedback on almost every essay in this book. Thank you, wild muses for helping me be brave and for giving me my best material.

For Philip Kain, who makes me laugh every day and is open to all forms of therapy, both traditional and experimental.

For Madeleine George, thank you for circling back and alternative kinship structures.

For Alex Baker, Arielle Greenberg, Caitlin McDonnell, Lynn Melnick, Suzanne Menghraj, Gala Mukomolova, and Karen Weiser, who prop me up with weekly texts, mini-vacations, Facebook love, and radical mothering.

For all of my artist, writer, and teacher friends who deal with my shit, love me, and show me the way through their own mind-blowing work and day-to-day living. Anselm Berrigan, Siya Bahal, Jacqueline Bishop, Nicole Callihan, Jill Dearman, Kristen Dombek, Diana Goetsch, Adjua Gargi Nzinga Greaves, Dia Felix, Jennifer Firestone, Ariel Friedman, Kate Greene, Grace Halverson, Joelle Hann, Ileana Jimenez, Rami Karim, Madhu Kaza, Erica Kaufman, Seth Loftis, Lisa Kron, Andre Lawlor, Katy Lederer, Brendan Lorber, Jessica Lynne, Dawn Lundy Martin, Rosa Mazzurco, Idra Novey, Danielle Pafunda, Jonna Perrillo, James Polchin, Theresa Sefnt, Sejel Shah, Amy Shearn, Laura Sims, Aisha Sabatini Sloan, Smoota, Leah Souffrant, Stacy Szymaszek, Michelle Tea, Amy Touchette, Rachel Valinksky, Nicole Wallack, Bill Webb, Simone White, and Aaron Zimmerman.

For Amy Touchette, who lulled me into my author photo with deep conversation and radical seeing.

For Alexia Saras, who cuts my hair and thinks I can get away with a fade.

For Rebecca Bull Ketchum, who taught me how to invert. For Miriam Wolf, who put me in full wheel.

For the Expository Writing Program at New York University and my mentors there—Barbara Danish, Darlene Forrest, Alfred Guy, Pat C. Hoy, and Denise Martone. hank you for teaching me to love the essay in all of its shapes and disguises.

For the Global Liberal Studies Program at New York University and the Institute for Writing and Thinking at Bard college, where I have learned to experiment, fight, and make my own way.

For my students. Thank you teaching me how to be present and writing with me.

For all of the pomoms everywhere.

For the editors, staff, and readers of the small journals that took the time to improve, publish, share, and read my work. I kept writing because of you! Earlier versions of these essays appeared in: *Aster(ix),* "Small Animal, Big Animal," *Brainchild,* "On Nitpicking and Co-Parenting," *The Establishment,* "The Jealousy Exams," "My Pills," and "On Portals," *GUTS: A Canadian Feminist Magazine,* "The Bloody Show" and "On Eating, *Linebreak,* "The Sick Book," *Mutha Magazine,* "On Unhappiness," *The Nervous Breakdown,* "21 + 21 = 42," *Public Books,* "On Spectacle and Silence" and "The Thread."

For Alex DiFrancesco, who swooped in to help with publicity.

For Molly Sutton Kiefer, my wise and intrepid editor. I really needed a home, so thank you for asking me to share my work with you. You don't know it, but the day you said yes to this book, I sobbed with joy and gratitude on a sweaty yoga matt in the East Village.

For everyone at Tinderbox Editions—Nikkita Cohoon and Jan Sutton especially.

For my agent, the brilliant and tenacious, Jesseca Salky, who is working with me on the next big thing.

For my mother who is always changing, for my brother who works so hard, and for my father who wanted me to be a writer.

And for Jamie Newman, who surprised me.

Carley Moore is an essayist, novelist, and poet. Her debut novel, *The Not Wives,* is forthcoming from The Feminist Press in the Fall of 2019. In 2017, she published her debut poetry chapbook, *Portal Poem* (Dancing Girl Press) and in 2012, she published her debut young adult novel, *The Stalker Chronicles* (Farrar, Straus, and Giroux). Her work has appeared in *The American Poetry Review, Brainchild, The Brooklyn Rail, The Establishment, GUTS, The Journal of Popular Culture, The Nervous Breakdown, Public Books,* and *VIDA: Women in Literary Arts.* She is a Clinical Professor of Writing and Contemporary Culture and Creative Production in the Global Liberal Studies Program at New York University and a Senior Associate at Bard College's Institute for Writing and Thinking. She lives in New York City. Visit her on the web at www.carleymoore.com